Cambodia

TOPOGRAPHICS

Cambodia

Michael Freeman

REAKTION BOOKS

Published by Reaktion Books Ltd
79 Farringdon Road, London EC1M 3JU

www.reaktionbooks.co.uk

First published 2004

Copyright © Michael Freeman 2004

All rights reserved.
No part of this publication may be reproduced, stored in a retrieval
system or transmitted, in any form or by any means, electronic,
mechanical, photocopying, recording or otherwise, without the prior
permission of the publishers.

Printed and bound in China

British Library Cataloguing in Publication Data

Freeman, Michael, 1945-
    Cambodia. - (Topographics)
    1. Cambodia - History 2. Cambodia - Description and travel
    3. Cambodia - Civilization
    I. Title
    959.6'042

ISBN 1 86189 186 5

Contents

1 Chenla the Rich: Land, People, History

'Most expensive fish ponds in the world', Roger said. He gestured with his chin through the window of the Antonov, now cruising noisily at about 15,000 feet. From the seat behind him I looked down. The light was failing, but a little to the side of the flight path I could see clusters of round ponds, filled with pale muddy water, embedded in the landscape. They lay splattered in a crooked line over the more ordered pattern of rice-fields.

We had just left Vietnamese airspace, en route from Tan Son Nhut to Pochentong. August, the height of the rainy season, sheets of water glistening dully all the way to the horizon. The Mekong still some twenty miles to the southwest, the Delta now behind us. This was my first sight of Cambodia, in the company of a United Nations delegation with Cambodian security, and we were not particularly welcome. My neighbour, whose revolver was tucked into his waistband, was nudging my elbow; he was the Deputy Chief of Protocol. We made small talk in French, but the atmosphere on board was a little strained.

The fish ponds, now disappearing from view under the aircraft, were indeed costly imports, having been provided by the United States Air Force. The *matériel* alone was well over a $1,000 dollars apiece, being an M117 750-pound bomb, of which a B-52 carried about 90 on an average mission.

These 750-pounders were the workhorses of the Air Force's war effort. Nothing smart about these bombs – just 600 pounds of Composition B, the general-purpose explosive costed at a dollar a pound, packed into a 150-pound casing. Then there was the delivery cost, from Guam. You might also want to factor in pilot training and ground control, although the value of this was moot when, as happened, and probably here, the payload was dropped in the wrong place. The earth shook, some buffaloes and farmers were blown to bits, and there you had it – instant fish ponds. The craters had no other use.

B-52 payloads were dropped from 30,000 feet in patterns known as 'boxes', covering an area on the ground approximately half a mile wide and two miles long. Being caught in this, whether as the enemy or as a villager on the way to a wedding, was to be 'boxed'. The very first to fall on Cambodia had been to our right, some 60 miles to the northeast, on an area known to the Americans as Base Area 353. In the early morning of 18 April 1969, to be precise. They had triggered the whole sorry mess of Cambodia's most recent unravelling.

An hour earlier it had not looked so likely that we would be flying at all. It was August, 1989, and the day had started well, in Bangkok, where we had assembled at Don Muang airport, a dozen journalists, under the guidance of our man from the Vietnamese embassy. Almost every morning for ten days I had taken a taxi to the Vietnamese embassy to see Second Secretary Nguyen Van Quan in an increasingly frustrating attempt to get visas for Cambodia. I was with Roger Warner on assignment for the *Smithsonian Magazine* to report on Angkor, largely inaccessible since the arrival of the war there in 1970. Cambodia's consular representation was limited, to say the least, and visas could be issued in Moscow, East Berlin, Hanoi or Saigon. In practice, things were very much controlled by the Vietnamese, whose army was still in the country, but despite Quan's determined politeness, the bureaucratic obstructions seemed insurmountable.

The sensible approach would be to have visas issued in Saigon. But that would require Vietnamese visas, and with no evidence of a Cambodian visa, they were stonewalling. Our only communication channels with the Cambodian Foreign Ministry were one-way cables or hand-delivered packages, which could of course be indefinitely ignored. On top of that, we had no seats on any flight. As Roger put it, things were soft around the edges.

Then, one wet monsoon morning, things changed. Our fixer in Tokyo discovered that the consulate in Saigon seemed to have been notified of our visa requests. I called Quan to ask for a transit visa for the end of the week, hoping that he wouldn't ask for proof. To my surprise, he said: 'Why don't you go tomorrow?'

'I'd love to', I replied, 'but I can't get on the Friday flight.'

'I can help you', he said. 'Bring the passports and some open tickets now.' Quan's story when we met was that the previous night they had learned that a UN team, hurriedly assembled as a result of the Paris conference, was prepared to allow the press to accompany them. This was to be the first step in the withdrawal of Vietnamese troops, and the resulting international recognition of the government.

It was a relief to be on our way, even if it was in a TU-134 of Air Vietnam (one of its companions had crashed into rice-fields on the approach to Bangkok not long before, with no survivors). We landed at Saigon's Tan Son Nhut in the afternoon, all rusting and decrepit hangars, mothballed aircraft and Russian-built heli- copters, and were guided smoothly and painlessly through to departures, on to a bus and out to a waiting turbo-prop of Kampuchea Airlines.

We sat waiting until a convoy of cars arrived and the UN team boarded, headed by the Norwegian General Vadset. The General was visibly taken aback by the presence of a dozen reporters, but obliged with a press conference of sorts. Clearly, the Vietnamese had been playing some games. One of the Australian reporters walked down the steps to find out from the Vietnamese officials what was happening, and returned shortly with one of them, saying: 'I'm afraid this gentleman has some news you won't like to hear.' The news was that now the Cambodian authorities would like to issue our visas in town, and would we kindly deplane and fly tomorrow.

This kind of thing tends not to go down too well with journal- ists, and this group turned truculent. The timing of the unwelcome news, however, couldn't have been better. Vadset's aide Anwar explained to the official and to us that since there were no runway lights at Pochentong, and it was nearly five in the afternoon, we would have to leave immediately. No one moved. Anwar said to the official: 'Can we talk outside?'

Through the window I could see him being persuasive. Finally, the Vietnamese and Cambodians relented. The aircraft filled with Cambodian officials and we took off. There was more confusion at Pochentong, with one airport official demanding that no one type or do any work, because this would flout 'our sovereignty'. Hul Pany, my Protocol companion on the flight, promised to clear our entry in the city, returning an hour later true to his word. As my mediocre French was nevertheless the best in our group, I got to sign the papers for all of us, in triplicate, and we were turned loose.

In the morning we took *cyclos* around the city. These are Phnom Penh's version of the bicycle rickshaw, a civilized contraption in which the passenger sits in front and has a perfect view of the street and passers-by rather than the driver's trousers. But the overwhelming impression was of a city that was still waiting to fill up. From our hotel south of the Independence Monument we pedalled north up Monivong Boulevard, and the strangest sensation was the lack of noise. There were hardly any cars, just the hiss of bicycle tires. It was already ten years since the overthrow of the Khmer Rouge by the Vietnamese army and the restoration of some order out of the chaos, yet Phnom Penh was clearly not a normal city. The wide boulevards like this one that the French had built, and which in earlier times had helped to give Phnom Penh its colonial spaciousness, now exaggerated its partly unoccupied state. The Khmer Rouge had forcibly evacuated the city in April 1975, and it had still not recovered.

It had been even stranger a decade earlier, immediately after the Vietnamese invasion. The Khmer Rouge had made a special point of destroying symbols of the previous regime and of urban prosperity, sometimes in gigantic acts of vandalism. The large Roman Catholic cathedral was completely demolished, not just pulled down but dismantled, every last trace removed, so that what remained was a patch of grass in the city centre where cattle occasionally grazed. When Milton Osborne visited the site in 1981, he found pavements with mangled private cars stacked three deep, like a casual wrecker's yard. One wing of the National Bank, arch-symbol of capitalism, had been blown up, and as he wrote: 'for years afterward, banknotes from Lon Nol's

10

Bicycles near the Central Market, 1989

Boarding the train for Sihanoukville, 1991

defeated Khmer Republic blew about the capital's largely empty streets.'

Only three Western journalists were ever admitted to the hermetic Cambodia of Pol Pot's four-year regime, one week before the Vietnamese invasion in December 1978. Elizabeth Becker, representing the *Washington Post*, wrote about this stage-managed visit to see Potemkin Village, Cambodia, hurriedly arranged as the regime realized that it faced overthrow. Sneaking out of the official guest-house early the first morning, as she wrote,

> I met workers standing in small groups by the curb, waiting for trucks to haul them out to their jobs in the rice paddies or factories. Otherwise the city was empty. The sunlight bounced off the cement and buildings, turned Monivong Avenue into a white canyon . . . Behind Monivong, beyond the stage-set perfection of the boulevard, the city had been left to rot.

The Central Market had been planted in banana trees. 'Their fanlike leaves sprouted like feathers out of stalls and vending areas. No people were in sight.'

Our *cyclos* turned off Monivong towards the Central Market. Here in 1989 was life, in and around the huge, grubby yellow dome and in the surrounding smaller streets. The fashion in women's hats, which most wore, ran to bonnets in thick brushed nylon, and the colour of choice was pink, the combination bizarrely at odds with the climate. We continued to the Foreign Ministry to report our presence, but this, like many parts of the city, was empty. Totally. Perhaps everyone had gone for an early lunch. We wandered around the corridors and offices for a while, then gave up and left.

PHNOM PENH 2003

Fourteen years later, as I write now, the city is on its way back to some kind of Southeast Asian normality. Arriving at Pochentong airport on a Sunday morning, my first sight was a bumper to bumper traffic jam, heading *out* of town, the new middle class of Phnom Penh on their way to the beach at Sihanoukville. The novelty of this was sufficient, it seemed, to mitigate the journey, which would take most of the day there and back. Traffic, of course, transforms a city, particularly in the case of Phnom Penh which has seen so little of it, and while its wide boulevards can still handle the modern flow easily, there's the sense that the city's new car owners simply enjoy cruising around. The perfect place for this is the river front, and Saturday evening along Sisowath Quay is where the action is.

I sat having a drink in front of one of the small cafés, each the width of a shop-house. The Khmer owner had left to study in Paris in 1970, and so had escaped the horrors of the next decade. 'But I returned as soon as it was possible, and I opened this place eight years ago.' I asked him how he saw the future for the city and the country. 'Wonderful', he said, blinking his eyes and gesturing out towards the road and the promenade beyond.

A steady stream of traffic, Toyota after Toyota, saloons, flashy pick-ups with chromed rollbars and arrays of spotlights, Honda Dream motorbikes almost all with passengers, sometimes as many as four. On the river side of the road, vendors of all kinds were gearing up for the evening. The most ubiquitous were the food-sellers, who carried everything, including a lit charcoal stove in two panniers, balanced on the ends of a bamboo carrying pole. With a small wooden stool only a few centimetres high, they could set up a pavement restaurant in an instant, whenever they could find a customer. If the first customer seemed to enjoy the food, there was a good chance that others would be attracted, and a group of squatting diners would accumulate. Meals didn't last long, and the clientèle would disperse as quickly as it had formed; the woman hitched the panniers on to her shoulder, scooped up her stool and moved on.

There was a continuous parade of commerce. A woman passed by, straight-backed, carrying on her head a huge open basket, something like a metre in diameter, with no effort, its contents large thin discs of rice bread. Behind her followed a man carrying stacks of small bamboo cages, each containing a small

'Come on in', says the sign to a small café in Phnom Penh

bird. The idea was to buy one of these, release the bird to its freedom in the sky and thereby earn merit, a few more Buddhist airmiles. The bird would, of course, later be recaptured and resold. A municipal street cleaner in a loose green smock uniform was evidence of the new governor's plans to revitalize the city. Chea Sophara has been responsible for much of Phnom Penh's resurgence.

Cigarette sellers strolled around, each carrying a small custom-made glass box perched on a wooden stand. Customization is easy in Cambodia, where labour costs much less than manufactured goods. A more elaborate invention is the cake truck, one of which was parked by the kerb opposite. A glass structure framed with aluminium, it delicately overhangs a small truck chassis, crammed with bread and pastries, the proprietor sitting inside on a low plastic stool.

Further up the promenade a medicine show had just got into full swing. Loudspeakers had been lashed to the surrounding lampposts, and the seller had started his long preamble, an entertainment involving many helpers and actors that was at least half an hour away from the final sales pitch. At this point the crowd was deep and happy to be amused. Only later would they drift away as the helpers circulated asking for money.

More popular than this was a macabre little tableau a hundred metres further up – a dead body floating in the river. One of the crew from a moored ferry boat was attempting to push the body ashore with a pole. A small crowd soon gathered, staring at the bobbing corpse, of which only the hands and face were visible, and this was the catalyst for a swarm of others, who had no idea what the attraction was. It had the temporary effect of clearing the traffic jam on Sisowath Quay, as almost all the passing motorbikes and bicycles swung off on to the promenade to see what was happening. Indeed, Phnom Penh is at the stage of 'catching up', when anything new is an immediate magnet. In early 2003 the city's (and country's) first department store opened, containing Cambodia's first escalator. This was such a novelty that the Phnom Penhois queued to try it out, and the store had to appoint instructors to show people how to use it.

Phnom Penh still retains the charm of an old-fashioned colonial town (it definitely feels more like a town than a city), courtesy of the French architects and planners who laid out the boulevards and introduced grand houses and official buildings. There is even a unique and imposing example of Art Deco in the form of the Central Market, known popularly as the *Psar Thmei,* or New Market. Painted a striking yellow, the huge concrete dome with radiating wings was built in 1937. It is still home to jewellers, gold merchants and other traders.

More interesting still in its way is the Royal Palace, which to the casual visitor looks like a lesser, provincial version of the magnificent Grand Palace in Bangkok. Yet it was the French who designed this, drawing on the research that the École Française d'Extrême Orient (EFEO) was conducting into the art and architecture of ancient Cambodia. The similarity in style between this and the Thai building is no coincidence. From the nineteenth century onwards, the Thais imported Khmer culture in all its forms, notably through artists, craftsmen and scholars taken back to Siam as booty during successful military campaigns. The French, as part of their *mission civilisatrice,* were simply bringing it back. Being mainly twentieth-century concrete, it looks best from a distance, as reproductions tend to. The original structures, including the Throne Hall and the royal pagoda, had been in wood. Indeed, the oldest building by far is not even Cambodian. To one side of the modern Throne Hall, which now dominates the compound, and next to the palace offices, is an incongruous structure in cast iron and glass, with a domed clock tower. This ornate French pavilion was formerly used by Empress Eugénie on the occasion of the opening of the Suez Canal in 1869, and was presented to the Cambodian king several years later by Napoleon III.

It was undoubtedly this Gallic enthusiasm for civic improvement and for the amenities that allowed the *colons* a civilized, relaxed lifestyle that made Phnom Penh so admired by all Westerners from the 1920s to the 1960s. This was a city that offered the comforts and style of a French provincial town embedded in the exotic and languid East, with its promises of

Entrance to the Royal Palace

discovery and pleasure. Here you could take a stroll along the Quai Norodom, a warm breeze wafting in from the Tonlé Sap river where it joins the Mekong, rustling the palms; then dine at one of the riverside restaurants such as the Margouillat; serving the huge local prawns and French wine. Or in the morning, coffee and croissants at one of the pavement cafés, perhaps a game of tennis at the Cercle Sportif. The white villas, where one could live in a degree of comfort and style probably unaffordable back home, attended by inexpensive servants, completed the Frenchness of the city.

For visitors, all this was very welcome. There was a handful of high-ceilinged colonial hotels, including the Royal, the Grand and the Oriental (these three 'under European management'), where one would arrive from a not-too-exhausting river journey from Saigon. River steamers plied upriver to Phnom Penh and then on up the Tonlé Sap to Angkor. In the 1930s they departed from Saigon three times a week in the late evening, working their way up the Mekong to arrive in Phnom Penh the following lunch-time, 'according to the current of the river'. The first-class fare in 1930, including food and cabin, was $27.50 per person.

All this was the infrastructure that provided the familiarities of home, from which one could make forays into a seductively alien culture. It did away with the risk and potential discomfort of really having to let go and enter a foreign society on its own terms. For the *colons* and other Europeans, Phnom Penh may have seemed to be in Cambodia, but was more an outpost of their own world. From it, they could enjoy both Chinatown and Khmer night life, which centred on night-clubs and dance halls, where at least half the clientèle would regularly crowd on to the dance floor to perform the *ram wong*, a sort of Cambodian conga.

But when it came to sampling the local offerings, the possibilities of sexual adventure were never far away. Buddhism, permissiveness and a basic commercial instinct ensured that pleasure was available without much complication to whomever wanted it – a situation that, it has to be said, held true in most Southeast Asian cities. With occasional periods of downtime due to war or political repression, Bangkok, Saigon, Rangoon and

Manila have all offered this. For Westerners, principally Western males, these cities have long been a sexual playground, inhabited by a compliant and available pool of talent. In Phnom Penh, according to the decade, girls have been available in *maisons flottantes* moored in the river, as night-club hostesses, taxi-dancers, gliding around the streets in cycle rickshaws, and more recently in grim little brothels on the road out of town.

At times, they seemed to be just about everywhere. I dined with some friends at a small French restaurant close to the river near Wat Phnom. Roland commented favourably on the selection of waitresses. 'Pour décorer la maison', the owner laughed, adding that they weren't much good at serving food. Jon Swain wrote of his first evening in Phnom Penh in 1970, when he was taken by a French friend to the Café de Paris, then considered the best restaurant, where, 'instead of emerging afterwards into a grey Paris street, full of passers-by hurrying with bent heads and collars turned up against the chill, I stepped into an enchanting world of tropical scents, the evening silence broken only by a bevy of girls in their cyclos who crowded round offering to spend the night with us'.

Part of the attraction was, and is, that prostitution here involves rather less soul-searching than usual, for both parties in the transaction. It also extends the range of services on offer, and in recent years this has led to Phnom Penh becoming a paedophile destination. The latest high-profile visitor in this context was the former rock star Gary Glitter, whom the Cambodian authorities deported after claims that he had taken up residence in the city for the purpose of enjoying young children.

Until banned in the 1950s, there was another exotic vice in which to indulge – the smoking of opium. This, like most entertainments with an Asian flavour, was administered by the Chinese who, as elsewhere in Southeast Asia tended to dominate city business. In French Indochina, opium was smoked in *fumeries*, a term much more elegant than the disparaging English 'opium den'. The most famous of these for thirty years in Phnom Penh was Madame Chum's. A certain cachet was attached to being admitted to this establishment, where one could smoke in the company of the city's business and social elite. The rituals of smoking included lying full-length on matting, head turned towards the long pipe that was constantly being prepared and attended to by a pipe-maker. It was also usually required that one change into a sarong, a kind of club rule with overtones of 'going native'.

Despite the problems of addiction, and the instantly recognizable drawn, wasted look of habitual smokers, opium has its knowledgeable enthusiasts. One was Graham Greene, in *Ways of Escape*, who claimed: 'Of those four winters which I passed in Indo-China opium has left the happiest memory.' His introduction to it seems to have been a revelation. As he described it: 'I could smell opium as I came up the stairs. It was like the first sight of a beautiful woman with whom one realises that a relationship is possible.' The madame, realizing that it was Greene's first time, limited him to 'only four pipes' so that the experience would not be ruined by the 'nausea of over-smoking'. Lucky Graham Greene. I tried opium twice, and each time felt nauseous after one pipe. I remember being told at the time that one had to persevere, and would eventually come to enjoy it. That seemed a poor motivation for entering a world that had evident drawbacks, seeing the pallid, skeletal appearance of old men who had conducted that 'relationship' for many years.

But the Gallic city of pleasure with its colonial architecture was a layer added to an old capital, founded sometime in the fifteenth century, coinciding more or less with the 'decline' of Angkor. In fact, very little is known of the period from the middle of the fifteenth century to the middle of the seventeenth. There are no inscriptions. The popular legend in which an old woman by the name of Penh finds a Buddha image miraculously floating downstream, and decides to build a stupa on the low hill (*phnom*) that gave the city its name, is just that – myth. The real reason for siting the capital here was its strategic trading position, at the confluence of the Mekong river flowing down from China and the Tonlé Sap from Angkor in the west of Cambodia.

There were no architectural splendours here until the French came – at least none noted by any visitor – but when the foreigners started to arrive they were generally impressed by the prosperity. At the end of the sixteenth century, San Antonio, a Spanish missionary, saw gold and silver, precious stones, fine cloths, ivory and a general impression of abundance. 'The nobles dress in silk and fine cotton and gauze', he wrote, and also travelled in litters. Regarding a recent skirmish with the Thais, he enthused: 'There are so many precious things in Cambodia that when the king fled to Laos, he scattered gold and silver coins, for a number of days, along the road so that the Siamese would be too busy gathering them up to capture him.' The trouble was that San Antonio, and most other Europeans following him, right up to the present day, formed his experiences from a very limited area – around Phnom Penh and another sometime capital close by, Oudong. In the sixteenth century this was the world of the court, the elite, other foreigners and attendant slaves. By the middle of the twentieth century you could add a bourgeoisie and subtract the slaves; otherwise the view was similar. What was missing was the bulk of the population, the rice farmers. Village life persisted, almost totally divorced from city life. Not even urban Cambodians knew much about the peasant society of the countryside, Europeans nothing at all, with few exceptions.

There's a sound a reason for this – the lack of roads. Even today there are very few paved highways, and most Cambodian villages are linked by dirt roads and tracks. Moreover, most of these are either very difficult or impassable from May to October, because this is a land whose rhythms are dominated by the monsoon. As in much of mainland Southeast Asia, there are three seasons that blend into one another. Beginning in about November, the weather is cool and dry, but after February it gradually heats up, until by April it is stifling. This hot, dry season ends with the arrival of the monsoon rains. Unlike neighbouring Thailand, Laos and Vietnam, however, it also receives the full impact of the melt-water swelling the Mekong river, which crosses the country from north to south.

Rice-fields, Siem Reap province, at the end of the rainy season

Net fishing on the Mekong

Cambodia, the size of England, Scotland and Wales combined, or the state of Missouri, has a compact shape, almost circular, and is configured rather like a saucer. The lip is a ring of mountains, most definite in the north where the Dangrek escarpment rises sharply above the plains, but also including the Annamite chain in the northeast that separates it from Vietnam, and the Cardamom and Elephant Mountains in the southwest. The forested highlands have always been the country's wild zones, populated, where at all, by tribal groups. The most remote, physically and culturally, are those in the northeastern provinces of Rattanakiri and Mondulkiri, bordering Vietnam. A frenzy of illegal logging in the 1990s wrecked large areas of the landscape, but this still remains best preserve of wildlife, and is home to what the Khmers call the *chunchiet*, or *Khmer loeu* – the hill tribes. There are more than thirty such ethnic groups, each numbering in the thousands and hundreds, including the Jarai, Stieng and Pnong.

The saucer's central depression is occupied by what is known as the Great Lake of the Tonlé Sap. This body of water makes Cambodia's landscape unique, because in tune with the monsoon it grows in size seven times between the dry and rainy seasons. The floodwaters swell the Mekong so much and so quickly that at Phnom Penh they back up into the much smaller Tonlé Sap river, which reverses its flow. Central Cambodia, a fifth of the land area, simply floods. The Great Lake covers almost 2,000 square kilometres at the height of the monsoons, rising from a shallow 1.5 metres to an average of more than 12.

Normal travel is completely disrupted, because in the land surrounding the Great Lake the largely unsurfaced roads turn to mud. Villages are cut off from one another; homes are isolated. Boats become the normal means of transport. Few other countries are so regularly fragmented for several months of the year, and it doesn't take much insight to appreciate what this might do to the society. Politicians, merchants, entrepreneurs and the middle class in the city are cut off from the large, normally silent majority of farmers, who eventually prefer to be left alone to get on with their own lives.

Yet the annual flooding brings an abundance of food. The silt carried down the Mekong is deposited and replenishes the soil; the water irrigates the paddy rice and supports an almost incredible variety of fish. On average, every square mile of floodwater contains a million pounds of fish, hence the Khmer expression 'where there's water, there's fish'. Actually, the full expression goes:

Mean tuk mean trei
Mean loeui mean srei
Where there's water there's fish
Where there's money there's women

or alternatively the last line can be:

Mean loeui mean avei-avei
Where there's money there's whatever you like

THE FISH HARVEST

Fish, anyway, are central to Cambodian cuisine. As the Great Lake of the Tonlé Sap swells in the rainy season, so too does the fish population. There are more than 300 species, and they supply about three-quarters of the nation's protein intake. One of the most delicious, and odd, is the *trei kranh*, or climbing perch. It's not a perch and it doesn't climb, but it has adapted marvellously to the annual cycle of flood and retreat. After the monsoon, as the Great Lake begins to shrink, the water levels fall and the ponds and rice paddies gradually turn to cracked earth. This poses something of a problem for the aquatic life, at least for those creatures unlucky enough to find themselves stranded in a small pond about to dry up completely.

The *trei kranh*, however, has adapted remarkably to this state of affairs. It is a member of the family of labyrinth fishes, so-called because of a labyrinthine chamber over the gills that allows them to absorb oxygen from the atmosphere. In short, they can breathe air in a convoluted fashion, and can survive out of water for several days. The downside is that they suffocate if held underwater, a hypothetical problem since there are other ways of catching and despatching them. As the dry season begins, the *trei kranh* start travelling – walking, or rather crawling, with a jerky gait, holding themselves up with the spines that protect their gill covers and propelling their torpedo-shaped bodies forward by wriggling their fins and the base of the tail. Searching for the next pool, they prefer to travel at night and in groups for safety, although this makes them an unusual road-kill on the occasions when they are caught in traffic. In one of the many Cambodian folk tales with animal heroes and villains, it is Trei Kranh who is delegated to set off and find the Wise Rabbit to recruit his help in saving the pond community from the Fox, who schemes to drain the water away with the help of the Pythons and so expose a large, sun-dried buffet.

Charcoal-grilled *trei kranh* happens to be a speciality at the restaurant of a friend of mine, Matthieu Ravaux, and it was here, in the shade of a grove of trees, that I first tasted it. 'Once', Matthieu said, standing between the tables, 'I found one of them walking through the restaurant, right here.' Inconveniently for the fish, it was heading for the kitchen.

The Khmer style with fish, however, is spiced rather than plain. Indeed, much of Cambodian cooking revolves around spice and herb pastes, known as *kroeung*, which roughly translates, as does its Thai equivalent, as the 'workings'. There are many *kroeung*, each one setting a distinctive theme for the dish, whether fish, chicken, beef or pork. Different combinations of herbs and spices are blended by pounding with a pestle and mortar, and the cook starts with this as a base. The ingredients can include lemongrass, galangal, tamarind, nutmeg, cinnamon, star anis, garlic, cloves, turmeric, ginger, kaffir lime leaves, cardamom, coriander, shallots, chillies and more localized leaves and plants from the forest. In good Cambodian cooking, whichever of these is selected for the *kroeung* must be fresh, and the paste itself should be freshly pounded.

Most visitors to Cambodia are already familiar with Thai food, and the two cuisines are probably closest among those of

Southeast Asia. Comparisons are inevitable. Very roughly, Thai cooking makes more use of chillies, in all their varieties from searing to intensely searing, while Cambodia is distinctive for the prevalence of sour and bitter notes. Indeed, the Cambodians distinguish four basic flavours – sweet, sour, salty and bitter – and perhaps have the keener sense of the divisions between these flavours. As a fan of bitter, certainly the least common flavour element worldwide, I have a special liking for the Cambodian approach to food. There are, naturally, many other differences between Thai and Cambodian, more detailed and more subtle, but these are better discovered one meal at a time. The two cuisines share an emphasis on fresh vegetables and little use of fat, making them among the world's healthiest. Rice is the staple.

As in other Southeast Asian countries, the cooking has absorbed other influences, and in restaurants you are likely to find two other cuisines encroaching on the Khmer – French and Chinese. In fact, while the chefs in the country's international hotel kitchens like to experiment, as they do everywhere else, and produce odd inventions under the heading of 'fusion', the authentic dishes remain distinct. Many Westerners easily confuse Chinese with indigenous Southeast Asian, not least because most upscale restaurants are owned by ethnic Chinese. The beginner's identification course starts with the cutlery. If the dish is meant to be eaten with chopsticks, it's Chinese in origin. If spoon and fork, Cambodian – and in the countryside you can use your fingers.

But then there's *prahok*, a paste that when used really sets the dish apart as pure, true Khmer. Yes, fish sauce is by now fairly well known – the clear, brown, salty, fishy liquid that turns up in a small container on the Thai and Vietnamese table as a pungent alternative to the salt cellar – but this is nothing like that. In fact, if you do consider fish sauce as pungent, then we're out of adjectives when it comes to *prahok*, which is a thick paste made by applying an ageing process to fish. One favourite restaurant of mine in Siem Reap, called the Hidden Flower, has a dish that they candidly offer in English translation as 'rotten fish'. It isn't really, although the smell would fool you, but it is made with *prahok*, and for that 'rotten' is a reasonable description. It's generally considered challenging for foreigners, so don't expect to find it in a hotel restaurant, and in truth it wouldn't appeal to anyone who prefers cottage cheese to ripe, runny Camembert.

But I feel I should speak up in defence of the world's rotten foods, for they're an endangered species: *natto* in Japan (fermented soya beans with endless strands of goo no matter how high you lift the chopstick-full from the plate), buried shark in Iceland, game in Britain. There, grouse, venison, hare used to be eaten 'high', having been hung for a week or two to tenderize flesh that was naturally tough from exercise. Much blander now, even at my local traditional butcher in London. The Khmers, thank goodness, are holding out against the tide of flavour mediocrity. I went to the market one day to see the range of *prahok*. At one stall there was a display of four blue plastic buckets, each filled with a different variety, all a thick, pale-grey, shiny paste, with bits of fish poking out according to which species had been used – a lump here, a section of spine there. *Prahok* is divided into a type made with just the flesh from large fish like *trei ros* and another made from whole gutted small fish like *trei kamplienh*, and further subdivided into *prahok* with and without the roe.

This is a way of handling the great fish harvest, preserving its food value through the leaner months, freezing not being an option. The first step, literally, is to squeeze out the oil, and in the villages along the banks of the Tonlé Sap that do this commercially, it looks rather like a traditional wine harvest. Supporting themselves on bamboo poles, the villagers stamp down the eviscerated fish in baskets or pits with their bare feet. They then rinse the fish in water and start pressing all over again. This can take several days until the fish are clean, at which point they are mixed with sea salt and packed into tubs, sealed and left to ripen. For how long? I asked the stall owner. 'About five months', she replied, 'until it has a good smell'.

'And which of these is the best?' I asked.

'Oh, this one', she replied, indicating one of the open buckets. 'It's made from *trei ros*. But also good is the *prahok kroeung*', she added, holding up a small clear plastic container with a screw lid containing a darker, smoother paste. This had had other ingredients added, including chilli, lemon and spices, and was intended to be eaten as a dip, used sparingly (yes, indeed) with plain rice. The industrial quantities on display were for cooking, as in dishes such as the 'rotten fish with bitter gourd' at my restaurant.

While we're on the subject of unusual foods, let's continue with what is best described as the comprehensive Khmer attitude to foodstuffs. Unlike the overly discriminating West, the Cambodians eat what can be eaten, and find ways of making it delicious. Frogs? Stuff them. Crickets? Stuff those also. If it moves, there's a recipe for it. On one of my first trips I was setting up the camera late in the afternoon for a formal shot of Angkor Wat. There was no one else around other than my friend Khon and our driver (this was before tourism). The camera was of the old-fashioned type, taking large single sheets of film, and to set it up meant viewing the image on a ground-glass screen and upside down, never particularly easy. We waited for the light. A little before sunset, all was ready, and I checked the ground-glass one last time before putting in the film. Something was moving inside, crawling over the image of the towers. At first I thought it must be a tiny ant, but no. I looked up. There on the central tower was a man, climbing. Curiosity about what he might be doing did not enter into it. 'For heaven's sake, get him off there', I said to Khon. Unreasonable of course, but Khon was used to my often strange requests. He and the driver started yelling at the man, who eventually did as he'd been asked and disappeared around the back of the tower.

When I'd finished shooting, I took an interest. 'Why was he up on the tower?' I asked, just as the man, by the look of it a local farmer, walked out from the temple toward us. He'd been catching bats. This intrigued me, and we arranged to meet the following day when he planned to return for more. What had happened in the twenty years since the French archaeologists had left was that bats had reinvaded the unattended monuments, and in their thousands. The five central towers of Angkor Wat, hollow and intact, had become bat condominiums, dark, spacious, perfect. Each day the famous sunrise view was preceded by a rushing sound, as if a sudden storm was blowing up – the return of these creatures to roost. The farmer had invented a technique for harvesting this valuable source of protein. With a neighbour's son waiting on the terrace below, he climbed the tower with a wire coat-hanger, hauling himself up the projecting antefixes from one level to the next. There were gaps between the stones, and with the wire bent into a hook he fished around inside until he speared a sleeping, hanging bat. Twisting its neck, he threw each down to the boy, continuing until he had sufficient for the family dinner. They were dusted in flour and fried with crushed garlic, he explained, until crisp. He was also, I thought, doing his bit for temple conservation.

I've always taken a professional interest in foods that are out of the ordinary, photographing idiosyncratic delicacies wherever I can find them, and in my experience Cambodia really does have the edge in one particular dish. I hunted it out recently. An hour and a half drive north from Phnom Penh on Route 6, the road forks. Route 7 runs east to Kompong Cham, Route 6 veers north-west to Kompong Thom, Siem Reap and ultimately Thailand. A cluster of buildings at the junction makes up the town of Skuon, of no consequence except for one speciality that puts it on the culinary map of strange foods. A little before the town is a short row of raised covered stalls and a restaurant, with a group of girls offering the usual fruits and snacks to passing motorists. A closer look, however, shows that some of the snacks have a disturbingly animate appearance. There are trays piled high with black things, black legged things. Skuon's contribution to the snack market is deep-fried tarantula, caught from burrows in the surrounding forests.

Ever so slightly sweet, garlicky and crunchy, the spiders combine the chitinous texture of insects with the weight and substance of something like . . . I was trying for a long time to find the comparison, and it recently occurred to me that they really do resemble soft-shelled crabs, and we know how popular those are. Well, if you keep your eyes closed. There's no special technique in eating them. Hold delicately by one leg (plenty of these to go

Arach-snack: edible tarantulas, one cooked, one waiting

round, of course), and bite into a leg on the opposite side. The crunchiness is pleasant enough, but the slightly gooey interior of the abdomen demands some familiarity and prior enthusiasm.

To be honest, I could not identify a distinctive flavour, but as throughout Asia, two other qualities come into play – texture and a belief in medicinal value. There is an idea that the spiders are good as a pick-me-up. 'If you're feeling tired and worn out', one man explained, 'these will give you back energy'. My driver certainly thought so, and bought a small bag of four to take back to Phnom Penh, for 250 riels each, or 6 cents.

Few Western readers will need persuading that this is all a bit odd, not to mention slightly stomach-churning. However, even in the context of a sub-continent where all kinds of insects are consumed, there is still a puzzle here. How and why did the idea of hunting for spiders as food get started? I read an attempt by an Associated Press journalist to relate it to the Pol Pot years, but since this species is *Haplopelma Albostriatus*, *aka* the Edible Tarantula since 1882, that doesn't work. The popularity, however, is recent, within the last decade according to one local seller, a woman in her early thirties. In general, insects get to be a part of the human diet for reasons of poverty and poor crops. The drought-stricken Khorat plateau north of here is a good example. The Khmer and Lao population supplement their food by foraging, and the catch includes ants' eggs, cockchafers, grasshoppers, lizards, small frogs, field crabs and so on.

The central rice plain of Cambodia, however, is a different matter. Watered and silted annually by the rivers, this is the nation's food bowl. Skuon, however, has forest nearby. 'Wherever there's forest', said the woman, 'you can find spiders', and she offered to show me some burrows. 'All the villages around here collect them. When people have spare time from the fields, they go out hunting.' She bought them daily from the villagers, who on average, she said, find three or four a day.

She explained the cooking procedure carefully. 'First', she explained, 'kill the spider', and showed me how. She pulled one agile creature from a blue plastic bag stuffed with a few dozen companions and a handful of leaves. Turning it over, she placed her thumb over the centre of the thorax, and, with her forefinger on the opposite side, squeezed hard. A slight quiver and that was that. If you try this at home, you will of course already have taken the precaution of removing the spider's fangs, otherwise you are in for 'two nights and two days' of excruciating pain, swelling and fever. 'And you cry', my driver added unnecessarily.

This prompted a general discussion about spider bites among the several people who had gathered around. Not everyone, it seemed, suffered the same. Some people were relatively immune, others had a very bad time. Nevertheless, all the spider catchers make sure to snip off the fangs with scissors.

Back to the kitchen. Wash the spiders, then toss them in a mixture of MSG, sugar and salt. No quantities given, but more or less a generous pinch of each per arachnid. Then crush several cloves of garlic with the flat of a blade (Cambodian garlic is relatively small), heat a quantity of oil in a pan, fry the garlic until it gives off a good smell, and then add the spiders. They are done to perfection when the legs are almost completely stiff, by which time the contents of the abdomen are not so runny. The drink of choice with which to wash this down (or keep it down) is clearly the national brand, Angkor beer, although my driver added, '*Any* beer'.

Oddities such as these, and the regular fish, chicken and pork, furnish the protein that supplements Cambodia's staple, rice. Throughout Southeast Asia, and in Cambodia in particular, rice dominates the diet to an extent far beyond that of any Western staple. The Khmer expression for eating is to 'eat rice', as if anything else for a meal would be unimaginable. It too depends on the annual floods, for as long as the crop has an abundance of water during the growing season it can grow on even poor soil. 'Rice', as one historian put it, 'is the solid rock on which Southeast Asian civilizations were founded.' And this now-small and impoverished country produced the greatest empire of all. At its height, with Angkor as its capital, the Khmer empire ruled almost the entire mainland, including what is now Thailand, Southern Laos, central and southern Vietnam.

Transplanting rice, Siem Reap province

The ethnic origins of the Khmer remain conjecture, not least because the history of settlement goes far back into prehistory. By comparison, the Thais and Vietnamese, who both migrated to the region from southern areas of China, are brand new arrivals. The first account of a Khmer kingdom was from Chinese emissaries of the Wu empires, who first visited the region in the third century AD and found what they considered to be a significant kingdom in the Mekong Delta. Whether the area was in fact unified under one ruler, or simply an association of principalities, is not known, but for Chinese purposes it amounted to much the same thing, because Funan, as the emissaries called it, was able to send more than 25 diplomatic missions to China between the third and seventh centuries, with tribute. The gifts included gold, silver, ivory, elephants and rhinoceros, and the plumage of kingfishers. In 1941 the French archaeologist Louis Malleret excavated a 450-hectare ancient city at Oc Eo on the Delta coast and found clear evidence that this had been an active trading port at the time of the Chinese visit in the third century. This included seals in semi-precious stone depicting bearded Mediterranean figures, and Roman coinage. What kind of civilization this trading port represented is still unknown.

The next suggestion of a Khmer kingdom also comes from Chinese accounts – Chenla. In the sixth century they identified two kingdoms, one in the Delta, which they called 'Water Chenla', the other further up the river in what is now southern Laos, which they referred to as 'Land Chenla'. Chinese accounts, however, are not as reliable as they could be. First, chroniclers repeated old accounts uncritically and as if the reports were fresh. Second, what mattered most was tribute sent to China, and the writers tended to embellish descriptions to make these barbarian states seem more important.

This made an attractive package of Cambodian history. First Funan, succeeded by Chenla (more powerful, bigger area), followed by Angkor (full flowering of Khmer civilization). Many people bought into this neat sequence, not least modern

Cambodians. The idea of a burgeoning greatness over many centuries, something that with effort and determination could be returned to in the modern world, had a considerable appeal. At the beginning of the 1970s, when Sihanouk was overthrown and the war began in earnest, the new Khmer Republic found it particularly attractive. The two major military operations of the new government against the Vietnamese in late 1970 and early 1971 were called 'Chenla I' and 'Chenla II'. The Republic's leader, the mystic, racist, palindromic Lon Nol, wrote an extraordinary chauvinistic tract called *Le Neo-Khmerism*, in which he interpreted Cambodia's time of greatness: 'At the peak of its splendour, our country earned the surname of Chenla the Rich and the people lived an easy, comfortable life. This sweet life was forgotten by the menace of war, and the Khmer people, after having known a period of glory and peace, were invaded by the Siamese in the fourteenth century.' And so on.

As it turned out, Lon Nol's troops were no stronger than had been the original Chenla. Claude Jacques, my colleague on two books about Angkor, is a leading Khmer epigrapher, and is rather dismissive of the Chenla idea and its implications. Working from inscriptions, he finds 'evidence in the Khmer country of a multitude of little realms and princedoms; those which the Chinese called Funan and Chenla, on grounds unknown so far, were among them . . . '.

Solid Cambodian history begins with the inscriptions to which Claude has devoted his career, and the first known is from the seventh century AD. In fact, Cambodian literature begins with these stone inscriptions. *Aksarsastra* is the Khmer equivalent of 'literature', from the root *aksar*, which means letter, or script. By any standards, Khmer script is strikingly beautiful, and complex. It reveals an elegance and intricacy that is almost a work of art. With the predilection for piling consonants on top of one another, each letter or script has a simplified form so that when one consonant follows another, the second is written underneath as a subscript. The Khmers call these consonants 'feet', and even though a couple of them are shared, this more or less doubles the written forms to 64. And, as the two dozen vowels and

Angkorean inscription at Preah Khan

diphthongs have different sounds according to which series of consonants they follow, they are written in two ways. As if this were not enough, twelve of the vowels also occur independently and look totally different when written. All this gives an alphabet of a staggering 124 'letters', with eight special signs thrown in for good measure. This rich complexity, what one philologist calls the 'genius and beauty of Cambodian writing', clearly developed in a society more sophisticated than villages and rice-fields. In its way the Khmer language, like the ruins of Angkor, reveals a history of past greatness.

In their endless rivalry with the Thais, Cambodians like to point to the script, claiming that Thai derives from Khmer. What is not in dispute is that the Thais themselves arrived in Southeast Asia later, trickling down from China mainly during the twelfth and thirteenth centuries, and that Thai writing developed after their arrival. The Thai story is neat and uncomplicated: King Ramkamhaeng, the first great ruler at Sukhothai, simply invented it in 1283. That, at least, is what he claimed in an inscription, part of which reads 'formerly, the Thai had no script. It is in s'aka 1205, the year of the goat [that is, 1283] that King Ramkamhaeng sent for a master who knew how to create the Thai script. It is he who we owe for this today.' Most Thais take this at face value. In *A History of Thailand* published by Chulalongkorn University (1977), Rong Syamananda puts the standard view: 'Realizing the importance of the national language as a unifying force of his people as well as a symbol of their independence, he created in 1283 the first Thai alphabet, using as its basis the Mon and Khmer scripts . . . evidently this monumental work testifies to his scholarship.'

There are two problems with this. The first is that it would be the only language in the world to acquire its script in one go. The second is that in fact many of the letters in Thai and Khmer are identical. And Khmer inscriptions can be traced back to the fifth century AD, with obvious similarities to a South Indian script. Worse still from the Thai point of view, quite a number of the Thai consonants are written just as the Khmer subscript, meaning that they come not only from the simplified, less elegant form, but from a 'foot' consonant – and in a Buddhist culture where the head is the highest and the feet the lowest, most impure part of the body, this is not a very good thing. Thais tend not to be amused by this, but the Cambodians chalk it up as a win.

The spoken language is no easier. European vowels are of little use in getting to grips with the strange but engaging sound of Khmer, and the only practical advice is to learn from a native speaker. And as for those stacked consonants, just try saying the word for 'tasty' in any way you can – *chhnganh*.

Just as the Thai script was not dreamt up one day by a king in a flash of inspiration, Khmer letters evolved from elsewhere – India. No understanding of Cambodia is possible without getting the Indian connection in the right perspective. The Indianization of the Khmers began many centuries before Angkor, but took place without dates, events or conquests. It probably followed a long period of trading, and, for reasons that are unknown, the Khmers willingly absorbed Indian customs, as well as script and religion, to the point where they help to set Cambodia apart, in appearance, from its neighbours. As David Chandler, Cambodia's pre-eminent historian, says, the process 'made Cambodia an Indian-seeming place'. Even in the nineteenth century, Cambodian peasants tended to dress like Indians, wore turbans and carried things on their heads. And one of the commonest sights of all in the country is a farmer with his small herd of cattle – familiar to Western eyes, but almost unknown among Cambodia's neighbours.

Above all, there is Angkor, national symbol and Cambodia's relic of greatness. Without Indianization it would never have been built. Everything from the iconography to the building methods comes from Indian models. Which is not to say that the monumental architecture and powerful sculpture are copies. Far from it, for the most compelling evidence of Khmer artistic genius is that they took the Indian inspiration and turned it to suit their own, uniquely Khmer tastes. Some ideas that in India were only partly realized were taken at Angkor to a much fuller conclusion. The most striking example of this was the attempt to create a working microcosm of the universe – actually several, by

Angkor Wat from the east. The entrance causeway is at top right

different kings, the largest and most intricate being the temple-city of Angkor Wat. The deity honoured here was Vishnu, and the universe being modelled was the Hindu one.

Actually, Hindu and Buddhist cosmologies are substantially similar, meaning that the two views of the universe, from hell to the world of men to the home of the gods, look very similar. For the Hindus there is a central continent surrounded by alternating seas and mountain ranges, all arranged in rings, concentrically. The centre of the continent, where we live, rises in its centre to Mount Meru – the world mountain, as it were, and dwelling place of the gods. In detail, the mountain has five peaks in a quincunx, like the five on a die, one principal in the centre surrounded by four at the corners.

Earthly representations of this universe are particularly useful, because they establish a cosmic link straight upwards. The Khmers worked this out very carefully. By building this connection, microcosm to macrocosm, the Khmer kings could tap into divine protection, always good when it came to the rice crop, general prosperity, defeat of enemies and staying in power. Angkor Wat was the most perfect realization of this, a fully functioning model of the universe in stone. Small by cosmic standards, but still not bested on this planet. In volume it approximates the Great Pyramid of Cheops, except that it's all carved, and is laid out in the centre of a city of 82 hectares. Surrounding everything is a broad moat – one of the concentric seas. Within this is a series of enclosures, each ringed with a wall or gallery – again, seas and mountain ranges. The temple proper then starts to rise in stages towards the middle, with its 42-metre-high central tower. This is, in fact, a temple-mountain, and at the very heart, rising above everything, are the five towers, the five peaks of Mount Meru. The carvings support the story, not least the almost 2,000 *apsaras* in bas-relief. These celestial nymphs, handmaidens of the gods and very obviously erotic dancers, were among the more tangible benefits awarded gods, just men and heroes fallen in battle. In Sanskrit they were also called 'daughters of pleasure'. Where there are *apsaras*, you have heaven. Well, a male heaven, anyway.

All of this makes Angkor Wat the centre of the universe. And the very centre of the centre is the core of the central tower, as we discovered one night, my friend Chris Burt very nearly terminally. It was one of the rare occasions when nobody was looking after the temples and very few people were there in any case. There were four of us, including Chris, Danny and Khon. As there was a full moon, it seemed appropriate to explore a completely deserted Angkor Wat. We had a bottle of champagne, half a bottle of Grand Marnier, and some of that Cambodian ganja so freely and more-or-less legally available (indeed, it had been the Chief of Press Bureau who had organized the purchase for us in the market, making sure that the half-kilo we bought was neatly rolled into a stack of joints). This altered, or rather heightened, our perception, and after gazing at the towers from the corner of the second enclosure we agreed to split up, explore individually and report back in an hour. I headed for the central sanctuary at the top, which was the base of the central tower. Nowadays the niches on each of the four sides are occupied by standing stone statues of the Buddha, but in the twelfth century any images would have been of Vishnu, to which the temple was dedicated (Claude Jacques, my mentor in these matters, believes that the large statue now in the western entrance gate was installed here).

For some reason I thought it would be a good idea to look behind one of the statues. At the time, it surprised me that I hadn't thought of this before. There was, after all, a space of some kind behind all four statues. Ordinarily, I would have balked at clambering behind a Buddhist statue backed up against the wall (and it wouldn't have been allowed by the guards, in any case). Now, at night, and with no one else around, it seemed an obvious thing to do. And behind was . . . an open doorway. I stepped inside, aiming my torch forwards. It lit nothing apart from some packed earth at my feet. The other thing that the light did was to create a whooshing sound from above. I shone the torch upwards. It caught small flickering shapes. I could gradually work out what I was looking at – the hollow core of the central tower, where bats had been disturbed by my entry.

I examined the ground more carefully. The interior of the tower was about 5 metres across, and the hard earth from just inside the lip of the doorway sloped down worryingly into a kind of abyss. It looked as if after a few steps you would simply slide on down. And this was, I reminded myself, the very centre of the cosmos, so probably better not to mess around with it. This pit, which dropped 25 metres to the level of the ground, was excavated by the French in 1934, but the only treasures found were two leaves in gold. Anything more serious, as might have been expected at the heart of this major temple, must have been looted centuries ago.

We reconvened, Danny having experienced one of the corner towers as a rearing cobra (it does look like that in silhouette), but the centre of all things seemed the way to go. We climbed to the tower and crawled around to the hidden doorway. It was a hit. Everyone was impressed, Chris so much so that with a 'I think I'll just see . . .' he stepped forward. And downward. Danny had the presence of mind to grab his belt as he teetered on the edge of the ultimate experience.

ANGKOR AND EMPIRE

Angkor Wat was built during the first half of the twelfth century, contemporary with the beginning of Gothic church architecture in Europe, starting with St Denis and the cathedrals of Sens and Laon. This puts it in the middle and at the peak of the six centuries of the Angkorean period, which began, more or less, around the year 802. An inscription from the west, carved two and a half centuries later, states that a king by the name of Jayavarman II, living in the Kulen hills to the north of what would become Angkor, declared himself to be 'universal ruler'. Jayavarman II appears to have been able to have consolidated sufficient small principalities, possibly by conquest, to rule a sizeable piece of central Cambodia, as far north as Champassak on the Mekong river, now in Laos. He originally made his base near the Great Lake, but soon moved north into the hills, perhaps for security, before returning to build the first of the Angkorean capital cities. This was 13 kilometres southeast of what is now the town of Siem Reap, and called Hariharalaya.

His son, Jayavarman III, began the construction of a large stone temple in the centre of the city, in the form of a pyramid. Called Bakong, it set the pattern for the display of kingly power for the next three centuries. Of the 21 kings who ruled at Angkor up to the end of the twelfth century, eight built new capitals, some of them overlapping earlier ones. At the heart of each was the State Temple, a symbolic, tiered structure – in fact, a 'temple-mountain', of which more later. These and other temples, together with city walls and moats, are the tangible reminder of the power and wealth of the Khmer empire as it grew throughout the ninth to the twelfth centuries.

The succession of power was sometimes hereditary, sometimes violent. Jayavarman III was probably overthrown, by Indravarman I, whose son's later accession to the throne was also bloody. This new king, Yasovarman, decided to move the capital to what is now Angkor, building it around Bakheng hill and calling it Yasodharapura. As these successions, disputes and building continued at the heart of the kingdom, the Khmer rulers waged regular wars with their neighbours as they extended the borders of the empire. Indravarman I, even in his short reign of twelve years, extended his control north of the Dangreks on to the Khorat plateau.

But the increasingly important rival for the Khmers, the only one strong enough to pose a significant challenge, was the Cham empire in the central coastal part of what is now Vietnam. King Rajendravarman successfully invaded the Cham heartland about 950, and, according to the inscriptions, 'His brilliance burned the enemy kingdoms, beginning with Champa.' This was the start of a series of campaigns of increasing destruction, which the Chams were eventually to visit on Angkor. Meanwhile, in the first half of the eleventh century, the armies of King Suryavarman I pushed west to conquer the Chaophraya valley, then moved north, attacking states along the Mekong and its tributaries, near what is now the Golden Triangle on the borders of modern Thailand, Burma and Laos.

Throughout this period, conquest was consolidated by a network of roads connecting the distant outposts of empire, and regional capitals were built. Two of the most important of these were at Sukhothai, which eventually became the first Siamese capital, and Phimai (known then as Vimayapura), about 140 miles northwest of Angkor. The roads made it possible not only for armies to move, but for goods to be traded between countries as far apart as India and China. At the beginning of the twelfth century, Suryavarman II took the throne after a power struggle, and during his reign of more than three decades aggressively pushed the limits of the empire to their furthest point – by 1150 the Khmer empire encompassed most of what is now Thailand, the south of Vietnam, southern Laos and part of the Malay peninsula.

This was the peak of Khmer power in Southeast Asia. After Suryavarman II, there were increasing revolts in the provinces, the empire's resources were strained, and the Chams, more easily dealt with in the earlier campaigns, were now more effective militarily. In 1177 they attacked Angkor from the Great Lake, having sailed from Champa, killed the ruler (a usurper) and sacked the city. That might well have been the end of Khmer rule from Angkor, but for a prince who had been in exile. He regrouped the forces, and, after four more years of fighting, recaptured Angkor and defeated the Chams. Crowning himself as Jayavarman VII, he earned his place as Cambodia's most famous ruler by this victory and by a subsequent building programme that exceeded all that had gone before. There were roads, temples, universities and cities. His new capital was the Angkor Thom that survives today, and other cities, including Banteay Chhmar, in the west. There seems to be an almost manic quality to this building activity, with many shortcuts taken in the construction and decoration. Stones were often poorly dressed and fitted. Quantity and scale obviously took precedence.

Jayavarman VII's was the last great reign. After he died about 1220, there was no sudden collapse, but the extent of the empire shrank, and there were few new buildings. And a new factor came into play – the rise of the Siamese. As they migrated south into what is now Thailand, their power and ambitions increased.

It was inevitable that they would challenge and overthrow Khmer rule in Sukhothai and other provinces, and eventually they came to fight the Khmers at Angkor itself. Ultimately, they succeeded in defeating the Khmer army and sacking the city, in 1432.

For a long time it was thought that this, conveniently, marked the abandonment of Angkor and the establishment of a new capital at Phnom Penh. Neat and romantic though this sounded, there is evidence that Angkor Wat, at least, was never abandoned, and that the shift of Cambodia's centre of gravity was more likely because of different economic priorities. Trade in the region was becoming more important, and the new city, on the Mekong where the Tonlé Sap enters it, was much less isolated. Nevertheless, Cambodia's power in Southeast Asia was definitely in eclipse, a steady decline in the face of the two new regional powers, Siam and Vietnam. During the seventeenth and eighteenth centuries, Cambodia was steadily squeezed by its two neighbours, both geographically and politically. By the early nineteenth century it had almost ceased to exist. Siam had annexed the western part of the country, including Angkor, while the Vietnamese for their part attempted to impose their own culture, values and even language.

The Thai king, Mongkut, known formally as Rama IV, was fascinated with Angkor. By the beginning of his reign, 1851, it was considered by the Siamese to be fully a part of their territory. Indeed, Siamese military maps painted and drawn on canvas at the beginning of the nineteenth century, now in a royal collection, show no acknowledgement of Cambodia as a nation. Thinking that his subjects might benefit from seeing one of the temples at first hand, in 1859 Mongkut dispatched officials to Angkor to find one that might be suitable for relocation. The idea was to dismantle and transport it to Bangkok. They reported that moving an entire temple would be too large an undertaking, so Mongkut settled for two small towers from the temple of Ta Prohm. However, when the Thai foremen reached the site and tried to implement the royal command, they were killed by local people. Unwilling to give up totally on the idea of an Angkor-on-the-Chaophraya-River, the Thai king settled for a large model of

Model of Angkor Wat at the Grand Palace, Bangkok

Angkor Wat constructed in the palace grounds, built to one-fiftieth scale. It's still there, tucked behind the Phra Mondop library of the Temple of the Emerald Buddha. For good measure, Mongkut added a replica face-tower over one of the entrances to the Inner Court, although the faces themselves are cute and pixie-like in the Thai style.

THE FRENCH AND RECOVERY

Cambodia's change of fortunes, indeed survival as a nation, came with the arrival of the French. Southeast Asia in the nineteenth century became the field for playing out the rivalry between the British and French empires. Britain's ambitions east of Burma were commercial, those of France both colonial and commercial. By the early 1860s France had annexed the southern provinces of Vietnam, thereby initiating a guerrilla war that continued at different levels of intensity for a century, bequeathing it to the Americans. The possibilities of the Mekong river being a trade route to China sharpened their interest in neighbouring Cambodia, while the Cambodian monarch, Duang, invited their support against Thai and Vietnamese domination. The first French diplomatic mission, in 1856, was turned back because of threats to the Cambodians by Thai political advisors. They succeeded several years later with the next king, Norodom, by concluding a secret treaty. Thai influence quickly waned, and after King Mongkut's death in 1867, the French protectorate over Cambodia was total.

Recovering Cambodian territory, though, was not straightforward, even with French sponsorship and prodding. What, after all, was Cambodia? Until the nineteenth century, the idea of demarcating territory was not a particularly strong one in Southeast Asia. One persuasive explanation is that in rice-growing cultures, farming is so labour intensive that power rests more on the control of populations that on land. Conflicts usually ended with the forced relocation of large numbers of people, and this tended to downgrade the drawing of lines on maps. For most Cambodians, the 'natural' extent of the nation takes in the

Khmer-speaking population, which includes the 'Khmer Krom' living in the Mekong delta in Vietnam, and the 'Khmer Surin' just across the northern border in Thailand. While no one seriously entertains the idea nowadays of uniting them with Cambodia, they crop up surprisingly often in conversation.

However, one tiny bit of the 'Khmer Surin' area was recovered, although it took 60 years and remains a saga. It took the arrival of the British and the French in the region to introduce precision to national boundaries, and the French to insist that more territory be returned to its protectorate, Cambodia. They supplanted the Vietnamese interests on the one hand, and on the other recovered the western provinces of Siem Reap and Battambang from the Thais. But they also set their eyes on a small but historically significant promontory of the Dangrek mountains in the north – Preah Vihear.

The Dangreks form one of the most definite natural borders in the world, an escarpment of Thailand's Khorat plateau running west to east on the edge of the Cambodian plain. Yet the temple of Preah Vihear is one of the most important in Khmer history, having been built by several Khmer kings between the ninth and twelfth centuries. The French came up with the idea of demanding a proper survey of the national border, with the watershed as the demarcation. So far so innocuous, but the survey in 1904 was actually carried out by a Frenchman and a Cambodian.

Well, watersheds are odd things. On a map and from a distance they can look fairly straightforward, but on the ground and close-up they can be confusing. In this case, approaching from the northern, Thai side, the land gently rises towards the edge of the cliff, but a short distance before this, it dips before rising again. The actual border is just beyond this dip. Of course, this is still a nonsense, and the watershed is at the far point, putting the temple on the Thai side. But that's not the way the map was drawn. And the Thais didn't pay enough attention to this. When it came to doing their own mapping, in 1934, they simply put Preah Vihear on their side, and in 1940 openly took possession.

Gopura Three at Preah Vihear, with the Dangrek escarpment beyond

Both points of view have merit. From the Cambodian perspective, this is one of the most significant temples built by Angkorean kings and sits on top of a promontory jutting out over Cambodia. From the Thai point of view, it's the watershed that should form the border, and it is every bit as much theirs as numerous other Khmer sanctuaries (the Thais don't care to use the word 'Khmer' in the art-historical context, preferring their own label 'Lopburi', implying that *their* monuments are home-grown).

Left to themselves, it's hard to say how the Cambodians and the Thais would have sorted the matter out, but as it happened the Cambodians still had the French on their side. The Japanese poked their oar into this during the Second World War by championing the Thai cause as one method of keeping the Thais on their side. The Tokyo treaty of 1942 returned Preah Vihear to Thailand, along with other territory ceded to France. After the war, the French took up the case again, demanding its return to Cambodia, and over the next decade this soured matters between the two neighbours to the extent that diplomatic relations were suspended. Eventually the Cambodians succeeded in having the case heard at the International Court of Justice at The Hague, in 1962. On the Thai side, it was defended, although not very well, by Seni Pramoj, who later became prime minister. The case went against the Thais, on the grounds that they had not objected to the map of 1904 at the time.

The result is a strange anomaly. For more than 200 kilometres the Dangrek mountains overlook the Cambodian plain, an abrupt steep edge to the Khorat plateau and a natural border. This one projection, however, is Cambodian, and because the entrance is on the northern, plateau side, it is effectively isolated, a little island promontory. The cliffs below are steep and difficult, and the stairway up from the plains, which takes more than an hour of climbing, is definitely the tradesman's entrance.

The Thais, indignant though they were at the judgement going against them, had no alternative but to accept it. But that doesn't mean that they have to be good neighbours, and having lost the garden-fence dispute they have for the most part been churlish. Hardly a Thai thinks that this is just, and Preah Vihear is doggedly referred to by its Thai name, Khao Phra Viharn. National sovereignty, always a touchy issue for the Thais, has been compromised. One way to retrieve the situation is to downplay the ownership and take charge of temple visits – a nice little earner for the Thai tourist industry, too. Organize the approach, fill it with food, drink and souvenir concessions, fly a few flags, and with luck no one will pay attention to the mini-border crossing. The Thais have tried this more than once, but politics have a habit of getting in the way.

During one of the periods when it was officially sealed off, I found myself holed up in a drab new hotel in Surin, a Thai provincial capital a couple of hours drive away, trying to get access. In fact, I had absolutely nothing to do but wait. The only member of our small group who had any leverage at all was Professor Smitthi Siribhadra. This border area was under the command of the Thai Second Army, and they were certainly in a position to help – if they wanted to. A Ranger unit looked after the section around Preah Vihear. With barracks near the small town of Kantharalak, they had locally recruited Khmer-speaking soldiers for liaison and some relationship with the temple's Cambodian garrison, the nature of which we were about to get some inkling.

The issue mainly revolved around whether I, as a non-Thai, could go. The day passed slowly. It seemed that the colonel with whom Smitthi was negotiating at the base had left for somewhere with his commanding officer by helicopter. No one knew when he would return. I called my friend Siriporn in Bangkok. She said that something was up politically, and that the army was involved. The rumours, as usual, were flying around.

In the evening, Smitthi returned from Second Army to say, rather to my surprise, that the colonel had returned and had agreed; I could go. We left the next morning and drove to the small town of Kantharalak, 36 kilometres from Preah Vihear. There we checked in at the Ranger barracks, where we had been given a dormitory. The Rangers had already begun negotiations with the Cambodian unit at the temple, but not without difficulty. There was a forward Ranger base at Maw-I-Daeng in radio contact with the barracks, but their contact with the Khmers was strictly face to face, and that meant that someone had to go on foot halfway up the kilometre-long series of steps and causeways. It was a tiring trip in the heat, and it had to be made several times during the day. Part of the difficulty was that the Khmer commander, a captain, was absent, and the negotiations to visit were going slowly, one step at a time. While we were having lunch, the captain returned and promptly said no, we could not go. The Rangers explained to us that he was a new commander, given to changing his mind, and considered 'difficult' by the Thais.

The relationship between the Khmers and the Thais here, conducted exclusively through these units, was a little odd. They cooperated by necessity, but there was an underlying political tension. Most of the northern plains of Cambodia, stretching out below the cliff-top temple as far as the eye could see, were controlled by the Khmer Rouge in this year, 1991, and the military outpost at the temple was relatively isolated. Understandably, these government troops were watchful and nervous, particularly since everyone knew that certain Thai army factions were actively supporting the Khmer Rouge, resupplying Chinese arms. Despite the obvious resentment that the government soldiers here must have felt, they also depended on the Thais for supplies, medical assistance and so on. The Thais were playing both hands, but by simple force of circumstance they had a considerable influence over the small Preah Vihear outpost.

The Thais were itching to open things up, seemingly less for political advantage than to make some tourist money. Each day a stream of Thai tourists in coaches and cars would drive down as far as the viewing pavilion at Maw-I-Daeng, a hill that gave an unsatisfactory glimpse of bits of causeway and stone pavilions, hardly visible through the trees even with the binoculars provided. The Rotary Club of Kantharalak had recently put up a prominent Welcome sign right next to the border, but still the Cambodian wouldn't play ball. They did not want Thais wandering around their defensive positions, and they didn't fancy the repercussions of land-mine victims – and mines were all around.

In the late afternoon, this is where we found ourselves – the viewing pavilion – while a Ranger staff-sergeant set off again for the Khmer outpost. Down on the plains patches of scrub were being burned. There was the muted thud of an explosion. Over to the left, about a kilometre away, a plume of smoke slowly rose – another mine detonating. Then, suddenly, everything seemed to be fixed. The staff-sergeant led us down the hill. At the last moment a Thai in civilian clothes – long-sleeved white shirt – appeared at the end of the road, carrying a camera, and caught up with the staff-sergeant, taking him to one side by the hand and talking. He appeared to be a tourist of sorts and wanted to tag along. The staff-sergeant agreed, and the man eagerly took one of my camera bags, smiling and bobbing his head. We now had a group of ten, a small expedition, and set off across the bare stone platform sloping down to a small stream.

We started climbing the first flight of ancient stone steps towards the outermost entrance pavilion – Gopura Five. A little way beyond this, by a small old reservoir partly filled with water, was the Khmer base. The captain did indeed seem a little strange, and certainly suspicious, but in the manner of being uncommunicative rather than downright obstructive. Still, we were free to go on up, a long, steady climb, up steps and pavements lined with boundary stones, through half-ruined stone pavilions. The view at the top, an overhang that drops away 500 metres to the plains below, was spectacular. In clear weather, although not today with the typical February haze as the burning of the rice stubble begins, the view is supposed to stretch as far as the Kulen hills.

To the left and right were the steep forested slopes of the Dangreks, controlled by the Khmer Rouge and the other two factions of the opposition. The government appeared to hold at least the immediate area of the lowlands, and for the soldiers here it was a hour's climb. Bullet and shrapnel holes pocked some of the walls, and mortar rounds littered the narrow vaulted galleries surrounding the now-collapsed sanctuary tower. The peculiar thing about this last sacred enclosure, I realized, was that it turned its back completely on the view. No windows opened outwards, and the only entrance faced back down the long axis towards Thailand. In the centre of the wall that looked over Cambodia, only a few metres from the cliff edge, was a decorated blind door. The Angkorean Khmers were fond of these devices, but they led nowhere, just solid sandstone.

About an hour before sunset, the Khmer captain appeared at the summit. He wanted us off the temple, right away, and we would have to negotiate the following morning all over again. After a night in the barracks we were back at the foot of Preah Vihear before dawn. By then the cause of our various little difficulties was obvious. At the roadside the man in the white shirt was there to meet us in a pick-up. Just before he locked the vehicle, he removed an automatic from his waistband and put it in the glove compartment. I wanted to kick myself for not having seen this coming, and with good reason, because we were no longer able to enter the temple. We waited by Gopura Five for the permission that never came. Eventually, the Khmer captain came down the steps with an excuse: his commanding officer was about to arrive. We didn't believe this but there was nothing we could do. As we learned later, the man in the white shirt was from a military intelligence unit known simply as '38'. Not a discreet member as it turned out. Up at the temple he photographed everything, including views from the cliff edge, which we had all been specifically told not to. Worse, he had asked the soldiers about the defensive positions and other details – and all in perfect Khmer. Except for this southern strip of the plateau, which is Khmer-speaking, Thais as a rule can't speak Khmer, and the Rangers have to recruit local men for liaison. In short, he stuck out like a sore thumb.

We returned to the barracks in Kantharalak for lunch, where the commanding officer seemed genuinely irritated by this turn of events, annoyed that his men had been used. As lunch drew to a close, I noticed some excitement at the other end of the room where there was a television. People started to drift over to watch the army channel broadcast. One of the senior officers returned and said, 'It's a coup.' The Thai government had just been overthrown.

56

It took only a few more years for Preah Vihear to open, and when it did the Thais flocked there in their thousands, daily. From the end, looking up the staircases, the stone steps were all but hidden by a sea of tourists, parasols bobbing, sowing a crop of discarded plastic bags. It couldn't last. The Thais were taking over again. The flag that flew high over the stone pavilion might have been Cambodian, but the newly swelled population was distinctly Thai. One government minister attempted to cut a profit-sharing deal with the Thais and was promptly sacked by Hun Sen. The deeper rivalry was not forgotten. In fact, far from it, because the Cambodians for their part started eyeing one or two of the other border temples, these inside Thailand, just. There was, for instance, Sdok Kok Thom in the west, just north of the Thai town of Aranyaprathet. Although not much of a monument, it was the source of an important inscription. Built by a senior court official, not a king, its stone *stele* not only laid out the status and lineage of its founder, but also gave the account, with dates, of the founding of the Angkorean dynasties. What is known of Jayavarman II is from here, so naturally the Cambodians see it as of national importance. Not that the Thais are having any of this.

The latest spat, though surely not the last, took place in 2003. At the heart of the dispute was Angkor Wat, no less. It began when the newspaper *Rasmei Angkor* quoted a Thai television soap star by the name of Frog as saying that she refused to tour Cambodia until Angkor Wat was restored to its rightful owner, Thailand. Few things could have been designed to incite popular chauvinist anger as much as this. Angkor Wat is *the* national symbol, and has appeared on all five flags since 1863, including that of Pol Pot's Democratic Kampuchea. And the Thais, of all people! Even so, no one anticipated the consequences, least of all the police in Phnom Penh. What followed was a night of violence in the city, with riots, the burning of the Thai flag and the torching and looting of the Thai Embassy, then Thai-owned hotels and businesses. The Thai diplomatic staff fled through the back door and the Thai military airlifted 800 of their nationals to safety.

Why anyone should have paid attention in the first place may seem strange to people from outside the region, but the basic issue is the increasing Thai cultural and economic domination, on several levels. One of the less important, but in this instance the trigger, is the entertainment business. The 1970s and '80s put paid to Cambodian film and television. Only recently has Khmer television struggled back to its feet (film has hardly started), while Thailand's highly successful entertainment industry does very well exporting to its poorer neighbours. Frog, or *Kob* in Thai, is a former ice-skating champion turned soap star, and is also the face of a Thai cosmetics brand called Miss Teen, another lucrative export to Cambodia (and not entirely unconnected to this case). The Thais, incidentally, use nicknames more than real names (the actress is Suwanan Kongying) and have no particular preference for complimentary ones. Frog, Fish, Bird, Chicken, Pig and Fatty are all popular.

No one bothered to check whether the 24-year-old Frog, who despite her name was quite a beauty, had actually made the remark. She vehemently denied it. 'I insist I haven't spoken those words or given an interview about it', she said, adding that the day after the riots was the 'worst day in my life'. The newspaper then suggested that this was a quote from the dialogue of one of her soap operas, but not even that turned out to be true. Someone had just appeared at the newspaper's offices with the report, and the story was put in unchecked. In other words, it was plausible, made good copy and was exactly the kind of thing that Cambodian readers perversely wanted to hear – more insults from their wealthy, tricky neighbour.

Events showed that the editor's judgement was spot on. 'Normally, the Vietnamese are singled out as the bad guys when it's time to whip up nationalistic fervour in Cambodia', said a Thai commentator, but Thailand is making an increasingly good substitute. Alone in mainland Southeast Asia it stayed politically stable after the Second World War. Indochina had its wars of independence, followed by Communist governments and worse, while Burma enjoyed a stifling military dictatorship. Investment and tourism flowed to Bangkok. Thai businesses exploited this dominance wherever they could, and until now Cambodia was an easy mark.

After the razing of the embassy, things went from bad to worse. The country's only independent radio station, Beehive Radio FM 105, broadcast a description from a listener claiming that retaliatory riots in Thailand had left ten Cambodians dead. Pure fiction, and the station owner was later arrested, but once again most Cambodians preferred to believe it. Even the Prime Minister Hun Sen, instead of checking the facts – or even attempting to calm the situation, for heaven's sake – joined in the protest by banning a broadcast of Frog's television show, saying that she was 'not worth as much as the grass that grows on Angkor Wat'.

And there, according to the opposition leader Sam Rainsy, you had it. The xenophobia, he claimed to anyone who cared to listen, was being whipped up for political capital. The police, after all, had done little to hold back the mobs and the fire-fighters had arrived too late to save any of the property. In a city, and country, where things like this are normally firmly controlled, and where orchestrated violence is not unknown, this might have a ring of truth. Did someone mention that elections were only five months away? Sam Rainsy, however, was denied a walk-on part when he flew to Bangkok to give his explanation. The Thai authorities detained him 'for his own protection', and put him on the next flight to Singapore.

Yet after all this, the closing of the border, suspension of flights, downgrading of diplomatic relations and deportation of illegal Cambodian workers ('I told the police to round them up and dump them at the border', said the Thai Minister of Defence), another story emerged. It was rumoured that a rival Cambodian cosmetics firm had planted the rumour in order to have Frog's Miss Teen range boycotted. Whoever thought that they were going to gain from it, politicians or businessmen, it turned out to be expensive. The compensations package offered to Thailand by the government came to 6 per cent of the country's foreign earnings. The progressive and popular governor of Phnom Penh, Chea Sophara, took the fall and was sacked. Someone had to; the Thais demanded it. Cambodia is learning just how difficult it is to become a fully fledged member of the fractious Southeast Asian community.

11 The Angkor Business: Restoring and Exploiting Cambodia's Heritage

In 1550, or possibly 1551, a king of Cambodia was in the area of Siem Reap just north of the Great Lake, on an elephant hunt or possibly a military campaign (this was a staging area for armies on their way to fight the Siamese). The vagueness in this account, written by the Portuguese traveller Diego do Couto in 1599, is indicative of the state of the country at this point in its history; even the name of the ruler had been lost.

The king was told that there were ruins in the area. Intrigued, 'He went to the place, and seeing the extent and the height of the exterior walls, and wanting to examine the interior as well, he ordered people then and there to cut and burn the undergrowth. And he remained there, beside a pretty river while this work was accomplished, by five or six thousand men, working for a few days.' This was Angkor, two centuries after the capital had moved south, to Phnom Penh. How much was in ruins is hard to tell, because recent research has shown that the temple of Angkor Wat itself probably remained inhabited as an urban centre into the fifteenth century. It seems likely that the clearing work under-taken was around the city of Angkor Thom.

Reportedly, the king decided to move his capital back here, but there is no evidence that he did, other than inscriptions recording restoration work at Angkor Wat. Additional bas-relief carvings, of poor quality, can be seen from this period on the north and northeast of the gallery walls.

But do Couto's account languished and was not published until 1958. Meanwhile, the reputation as the first Westerner to 'discover' Angkor had by popular vote gone to a French naturalist, Henri Mouhot, who arrived in 1860. The purpose of his self-financed expedition to Southeast Asia was botanical, but he was side-tracked by tales of Angkor that were circulating in Bangkok;

several other Westerners had recently been there. Why it should have been Mouhot that was credited with finding Angkor is largely because he wrote sufficiently well to be serialized in a popular French travel magazine, *Tour du Monde*, with the added romantic touch of his death a year later of fever in the forests of Laos (his final entry, 'have pity on me, oh my God . . .!', was in the tradition of explorer-martyrs). Ironically, as a Frenchman, Mouhot could drum up no support for his expedition in France, and it was with the encouragement of the Royal Geographical Society in London (but with no financial backing) that he left for Asia. His sketch map of Angkor is still there in the library, which until quite recently would allow it to be taken out on loan.

Mouhot sat on top of the Bakheng, gazing 'upon the wooded plain and the pyramidal temple of Ongcor, with its rich colonnades, the mountain of Crome [Phnom Krom], which is beyond the new city, the view losing itself in the waters of the great lake on the horizon.' He sentimentalized: 'Sad fragility of human things! How many centuries and thousands of generations have passed away, of which history, probably, will never tell us anything.'

Angkor tends to induce this in writers. A little hindsight should have suggested to him that archaeology, epigraphy and the other skills used to reconstruct ancient sites would furnish most of the answers, once serious exploration began. But the idea of mysteries too deep ever to be solved has a certain appeal, and it certainly struck the right note in 1863 with the readers of the *Tour du Monde*. The publication in the magazine and later book did more than anything else to put the spotlight on Angkor for the West.

Mouhot continued musing: 'All this region is now as lonely and deserted as formerly it must have been full of life and cheerfulness: and the howling of wild animals, and the cries of a few birds, alone disturb the solitude.' There is not much howling these days, because Cambodia's wildlife has had a rough time recently. Mouhot's experience was of forests 'infested with elephants, buffaloes, rhinoceros, tigers and wild boars'. He elaborated: 'We live almost as in a besieged place, every moment dreading some attack of the enemy, and keeping our guns constantly loaded.'

This is almost certainly embellishment to give a *frisson* to his readers. Tropical forest, whether the monsoonal variety here or the full canopy rainforest closer to the Equator, hides its animals well, and for most first-time visitors it gives an impression of being deserted. Forest life for the larger mammals tends to be secretive and quiet – even elephants, despite their bulk, can move silently among the trees, using their trunks to push branches aside, placing the huge pads of their feet with a surprising delicacy on the carpet of leaves.

The bird life is more obvious. With less visibility than in grassland or temperate woodland, song becomes more important for communication, and the tropical chorus is richer and more varied. But years of war and hunger have pretty well done for Cambodia's wildlife, much of which has ended up in the pot, and the process has been made much easier by the military weapons with which the country has been awash for more than three decades.

AN ANGKEAN BESTIARY

About a kilometre from where Mouhot sat overwhelmed by it all, the road runs past Angkor Wat on its way north to the twelfth-century city of Angkor Thom. On a cloudy August morning, sultry with the promise of rain, we drove along this road in an old powder-blue Volga, the broad moat on our right. The car had no air-conditioning and the windows were wound down; we heard a series of sharp cracks above the engine noise. At the same time a small flock of ducks wheeled high over the water.

A little further, as we approached the end of the moat, its northwest corner, I could see what was making the noise. A soldier stood on the stone parapet, firing in the air with his M-16. He was aiming at the ducks, with a predictable lack of success. A 12-bore shotgun would have been the weapon of choice were the ducks lower, but the single small rounds of the M-16 would have needed impossible accuracy. Eventually, no doubt, persistence and luck would triumph over common sense. Little wonder that the forests were largely silent.

Even so, Cambodian birds have fared better than anything on four legs, and are now right up there near the top of a distinctly shorter food chain. The best view that remains of the wildlife, oddly enough, is carved on the walls of these temples. I turned this into an idle pastime – a medieval bestiary seen through the eyes of Khmer sculptors, mainly from the eleventh and twelfth centuries. Stone-carving skills tailed off after this, but most of the bas-reliefs at Angkor display a very good eye for detail and accuracy, and occasional flashes of artistic brilliance.

One group of animals harasses sinners on the south gallery wall at Angkor Wat. Being dragged by giant demons to their appointments in the 32 hells, the emaciated unfortunates are set upon by a tiger, rhinoceros and two giant snakes. The tiger, its stripes elegantly incised in short, wavelike curves, has seized one man, dragged him to the ground, and is tearing into his shoulder. The rhinoceros, which has just up-ended another scrawny sinner, is exquisitely rendered, sufficiently to identify the species. There are, or rather probably were, two species of rhinoceros in Cambodia, the Lesser One-Horned and the Asian Two-Horned. The horns, however, are not up to much in either of them, and Two-Horned females have only a slight thickening of the skin behind the stubby front protuberance (not that horn deficiency has lessened the demand in superstitious Chinese medicine). The way to identify the species is in the number of folds of skin across the back and in its decoration, and here on the sandstone relief is an anatomically perfect One-Horned animal, with three folds across its back and a mosaic pattern.

A pair of similar rhinos appears on the opposite side of the temple, harnessed to a chariot ridden by the Vedic fire god, Agni. Although the Khmers enthusiastically adopted Indian religions and the Indian pantheon of gods, they suited themselves in the way in which they did this. In India, each god has a steed to ride, usually an animal, and Agni's is traditionally a goat. For some unknown reason, the Khmers preferred a rhinoceros from their own forests, and it certainly makes a more striking mount.

The giant snakes, rearing higher than the rhino, are as real in the Khmer view as any other forest creature. They are *nagas*, called *neak* in Khmer, serpent-genies from the watery under-world. As in other religious borrowings, the Khmers had their own take on things, and *nagas* were promoted. From India there were a few famous *nagas*, illustrious enough to have names, and these were duly honoured in bas-relief carving and statues. There was Ananta, also called Sesha – 'Endless' – a giant serpent that supported the sleeping god Vishnu as he floated on the Ocean of Milk dreaming the Universe into existence, a sort of serpentine lilo. Another gargantuan *naga* was Vasuki, whose body was wrapped around the swivelling, pivoted Mount Mandara so that it could be rotated to and fro in order to churn the same Ocean of Milk. A team of gods held Vasuki's tail and a team of demons the heads, pulling alternatively in a rare display of cooperation, all to release *amrita*, the elixir of life. The first beings to be created in this operation are the *apsaras*. And on a later occasion, to protect the meditating Buddha from a downpour, another *naga* of merit rose above the Master to shelter him with its cobra-like hood.

These were the great and the good of the *naga* world, but the Khmers were more than usually obsessed with these serpents, and at Angkor they are all over the place. They undulate down the edges of pediments over temple doorways, they rear up at the corners of roofs, and they line walkways as balustrades. They may occasionally have a single head, but more often three, five or even seven (always an odd number). The Khmers, in fact, owe their existence as a people to the *nagas*. In the Cambodian founda-tion myth, a Brahmin priest, Kaundinya, married a *naga* princess, half-woman, half-serpent. Their union began the royal line.

But back to the parade of temple wildlife. In processions and battles, the heavyweights are elephants. Unlike the African species, the Asian elephant can be domesticated, and until the twentieth century it played a full part in the history and economy of the region. Indeed, these bas-reliefs are the first Southeast Asian records to show elephants playing a role in court and mil-itary life. The Khmers may well have initiated the organized use of elephants in Southeast Asia, and on the walls of Angkor Wat

Marine creatures caught up in the Churning of the Ocean of Milk, Angkor Wat

Sinners being dragged to their punishment, Angkor Wat

they dominate the royal procession. A century and a half later a Chinese diplomat, the only foreigner to record life at Angkor, wrote:

> Finally the Sovereign appeared, standing erect on an elephant and holding in his hand the sacred sword. This elephant, his tusks sheathed in gold, was accompanied by bearers of twenty white parasols with golden shafts. All around was a body-guard of elephants, drawn close together, and still more soldiers for complete protection, marching in close order.

The practice certainly caught on with the neighbours. Elephants were not only useful; they gave status. And for a king, his elephants had to be special. Between the Cambodians, Thais, Laos and Burmese, the idea developed that in order to be a 'universal monarch', a *chakravartin*, you needed, among other things, a white elephant. There were other attributes needed, such as a wife, a son, a horse (no special colour), but these were fairly straightforward to acquire. A white elephant, however, was another matter. Why white? Hindu and Buddhist mythology presented two ideal examples. There was the elephant steed of the Vedic sky god Indra, called Airavata (who also had three heads, but on earth that was asking a bit too much). There was also, perhaps more relevant, the white elephant that came in a dream to Maya, the mother-to-be of the Buddha. Unfortunately, albino elephants, like most other albinos, are extremely rare, and in general Southeast Asian kings fudged the issue by concocting an arcane set of characteristics that would do almost as well. Elephants could be notionally white, even lightened occasionally by vigorous scrubbing, and it didn't matter that to the average ignorant member of the public these auspicious creatures looked much the same as any other elephant.

Cambodian elephants also fought. The place to see them is the Bayon, the state temple at the heart of Angkor Thom, the city built at the end of the twelfth century by Jayavarman VII once he had recaptured Angkor from the invading Chams. Leaving the duck hunter behind, we continued north, past the hill of Phnom

68

Naga balustrade at Preah Vihear, near Gopura Five

Bakheng. More recently, real elephants stand here in the shade, swaying slowly, with a howdah on their back, waiting to haul tourists up to where Henri Mouhot once sat gazing out over the temples. A little further and we reached the causeway, lined with statues of gods and demons, leading up to the tall gateway of Angkor Thom – the name means Angkor the Great. We entered and drove into forest. The tall trees, deep on either side, mask the fact that this was a heavily populated capital eight centuries ago, and stayed that way for more than 200 years.

After a kilometre and a half we reached the Bayon, directly ahead of us and looking like a jumble of rocks from a distance, only gradually resolving itself into an apparently loose arrangement of grey towers, rising towards the centre. The road encircles the temple. We stopped, parked and walked along the eastern causeway towards the mass, sharing the weight of the camera equipment. The gunfire of the duck shoot was too distant to hear; or maybe he had given up.

The entire outer wall is covered in bas-reliefs, not mythological but historical, showing battles and scenes from daily life. In the huge panoramas of armies on the march, scores of elephants plough their way into battle, some ridden by commanders, others carrying weapons, including enormous contraptions operated by two soldiers that appear to be large mobile crossbows. And at the western end of the south gallery wall are two others. Unlike the war elephants further along the bas-relief and the processional elephants depicted at Angkor Wat, this pair is not caparisoned. They have just a rope halter, by which they are being led down a slope, and the likeliest explanation is that they have just been caught and are being brought down the mountainside.

This might have been the Kulen hills some 30 or so kilometres to the northeast, but the nearest mountains and forests where there is a record of elephant capture is the Dangrek range on the northern border. On the Thai side there still remains a small community of Kui, an ethnic group renowned for its skill with these animals. Considered by most sources to be 'the original inhabitants of parts of Thailand and Cambodia, predating invasions of the region by the Mon-Khmer', the Kui made a

70

profession of capturing wild elephants. As noted by the leading expert on domesticated Asian elephants, Richard Lair, they have a special language used only when capturing in the forest – and only this language must be used on these occasions. Since 1957, however, the Thai government has not allowed the Kui to cross into Cambodia in pursuit of the animals, and in any case the wholesale destruction of the forest has drastically reduced the elephant population. One researcher in the 1950s recorded that the region was 'teeming with wild beasts, among them many wild elephants'. Now, once a year, the remaining Kui mahouts travel with their animals to the nearby town of Surin for the Elephant Round-Up. Since the Tourist Authority of Thailand took it over in the 1980s this has become a rather dismal circus with elephants playing silly games, but an echo of the real business remains in the demonstration of elephant capture. The Kui ride their *khoonkies* (elephants used to capture and train others) in pursuit of the 'wild' herd, cutting off one animal from the rest and lassoing it in their own unique way, slipping the loop around a hind foot.

Elephants have certainly come down in the world since the old days. From being a beast of burden they have become, in Cambodia, simply a burden. An Asian elephant eats on average 250 kilograms of food a day, and there are a lot of days in an elephant's lifespan. Lair's considered estimate of the domesticated elephant population in Cambodia is around 300, with the possibility of more being kept unrecorded by remote tribal groups such as the Phnong in Mondulkiri. The Khmer Rouge destroyed, among other things, the government records. A survey in the 1990s came up with a figure of 104 for Mondulkiri province, which probably has the largest population of the animals. Until the French owner of a hotel decided to set up an elephant conservation centre at Angkor, there was none at all in Siem Reap province. The Compagnie des Elephants d'Angkor had acquired sixteen animals by August 2000, with another six on their way from Mondulkiri, walking. They earn their keep by carrying visitors up and down Bakheng hill, close to where they live with their mahouts.

Ritual sacrifice of a wild buffalo, the Bayon

Another intriguing wildlife story unfolds on the east wall of the Bayon. High up, amid scenes of an army returning successfully from battle, a handsome, muscular bovine with wide, curving horns is tethered by the neck to a tree. One man holds its tail; another stands in front, holding one of the animal's forelegs with his left hand while raising a spear in his right. This is clearly a sacrifice about to be made, and a reasonable guess is that it is in honour of a military victory. Buffalo sacrifices were traditional rites to propitiate spirits among the hill-tribes of Cambodia, and here evidently among the Khmer at the height of Empire.

The method varied. Here on the wall of the Bayon, although the buffalo seems distracted by the viewer and appears not to be aware of its immediate fate, the weapon is a spear. I saw exactly this, long ago and way to the north, beyond Cambodia in the hill-country that separates Thailand from Burma. The tribal group was the Akha, and in a village on the upper slopes of a hill called Doi Thung the preparations were well under way for the funeral of an important elder. For three nights and two days the village shaman – its spirit priest and keeper of traditions – had been chanting the death rites. The execution was to take place early in the morning of the following day.

As the bright December sun cleared the ridge above the village, the buffalo was tied by the neck to a heavy stake. The entire village gathered around, one group of men standing close to the animal. The shaman approached with a short-hafted spear and a bowl of rice. Repeatedly, he sprinkled rice grains on three parts of the animal's back, then prodded the flank with his finger, chanting the whole while. The buffalo did not like this at all, and seemed aware that it was the main celebrant in a ritual that would have an unpleasant ending. The helpers, once the shaman had retired from sprinkling and prodding, were having difficulty goading the animal into the correct position.

The idea was to make a clean, deep thrust that would penetrate the heart and take the buffalo down quickly, just as in bullfighting. There are just two ways to do this. The more difficult is from the front, plunging the weapon down through the shoulder muscles; the other is from the side. In either case the problem is the shoulder blades, which shield the heart. Matadors naturally take the braver approach from the front, but here the shaman attacked from the side, to shouts of encouragement. His first stroke was a short jab, pulling back with the spear almost immediately. Nothing happened for a couple of minutes, and when it became apparent that the buffalo was not going to keel over and die, he returned for a second lunge. This time the spear was in the right place. For about half a minute the animal stood absolutely rigid, then began to shake. With increasing spasms running through its body, its legs finally gave way and it fell to the ground.

At this point, a surprising thing happened. The men who had been standing close suddenly rushed forward. Two of them twisted the buffalo's head round to face upwards, hard against the stake. Others prised its jaw open and forced a section of thick bamboo deep into its mouth, while another began pouring water into this, using it as a funnel. As this was going on, everyone else – men, women, children – was shouting, but in a controlled, rehearsed way, not spontaneous at all. The buffalo's shocked eyes bulged, then glazed. It stopped struggling.

This seemed an extraordinary thing to do to a dying animal, but there was a sound reason. The buffalo, which had been committed to the deceased and would accompany him, guiding him along the middle path to the land of the ancestors, could not be allowed to moan in its death throes. Finally, it was laid out neatly, its legs arranged straight, and covered in unhusked rice.

When Norman Lewis travelled in the Annamite chain that separates eastern Cambodia from Vietnam in 1950, he happened across a buffalo sacrifice in a Moï village, 'a distressing spectacle' on account of the drawn-out method of killing. Two men first started hacking away at the leg tendons to disable it thoroughly. Two others then approached with spears, but in contrast to the ceremony that I had witnessed, 'no particular technique, it seemed, was demanded of the killers, and they had a good half-hour in which to pursue their prey with desultory proddings and stabbings'.

74

Such are the archetypal buffalo sacrifices of Southeast Asia, and this was the scene reconstructed, with added drama, in Francis Ford Coppola's *Apocalypse Now*, of which more later. In the climax of the movie, set in a notional Rattanakiri Province in the northeast of Cambodia, the tribal warriors of Marlon Brando's private army behead a buffalo as Martin Sheen, the US Army assassin, performs the same on Brando.

The resonances are curious. Buffalo sacrifices are, according to David Chandler, muted echoes of human sacrifice, which undoubtedly took place in Cambodia until at least the late nineteenth century. The hill-tribe sacrifices of buffalo are animistic, but among the Khmers there is evidence that they were connected to the worship of Shiva's wife in a special form – as the slayer of the buffalo-demon Mahisa. There are a number of seventh-to-tenth-century statues and bas-reliefs of this goddess, one of them from the hills of Ba Phnom southeast of Phnom Penh, and there is a fascinating account taken from a local resident who lived there at the end of the nineteenth century, one Dok Than.

In front of the statue, Lewis relates, was 'the place where buffaloes are sacrificed' – to the ancestor spirit embedded in the statue – but a few hundred metres to the east was where humans were also sacrificed. The old man had seen one of these. After communal prayers, the executioner,

> holding a sword, danced hesitantly around the victim and then cut off his head with one stroke. The people looked to see what direction the victim's blood fell. If it fell evenly, or spurted up, then rain would fall evenly over the district. But if the blood fell to one side, rain would fall only on that side of the district.

By the beginning of the twentieth century, buffaloes were substituted for humans.

There is a puzzle, however, in the carving on the wall of the Bayon. I have an idea of the ceremony, but what kind of buffalo is it? With those magnificent horns and that elegant physique, certainly not a domestic water buffalo. It's wild, and there's no problem with that. Even as late as 1944 the French conservator at Angkor, Maurice Glaize, could write of herds of wild buffalo worth hunting. But the problem is that there are just three species in the region, and this specimen doesn't look much like either of the two most common. These are the banteng and the gaur, readily identifiable by, among other things, their horns.

The third species, however, really would be a prize – the kouprey, identified as a species only in 1937 and extremely rare. The centre of its range was the northern plains of Cambodia, but it has not been seen since 1988. This is not because the kouprey is inconspicuous. Weighing in at around 900 kilograms and standing up to two metres at the shoulder, this is a massive creature. But uncontrolled hunting during years of war, presumably for food, has reduced the population to . . . who knows? Maybe there is none left. The kouprey has certainly had a bad time with human armed conflict. The only specimen ever in captivity was a calf shipped to France, mistakenly as a gaur, in 1937. It survived just three years, dying of starvation at the Vincennes Zoo in Paris under the German occupation,

The kouprey has only been photographed clearly once, and that was a female, very different from a bull, with lyre-shaped horns. And the horns are the key, because those of the bull arch forward and upward in a double curve, as do these on the wall. Everywhere else we can trust the carvers' eye for detail, so perhaps here too. Could it be? Obviously wishful thinking on my part, but I still think it's in there with a chance. Sihanouk in 1960 declared the kouprey the national animal, a singularly poor choice of symbolism given that the animal was on the verge of extinction. The extinction thing certainly did for my favourite Angkor animal, a stegosaur tucked away inside the west gate at Ta Prohm . . . not bad for thirteenth-century imagination, right down to the diamond-shaped dorsal plates across its back, diminishing in size down to the tip of its tail.

And yet, amid all the gloomy forecasts for Cambodia's real wildlife, there was an unexpected piece of good news in 2000. Biologists from the World Wildlife Fund and the Wildlife

Conservation Society at the Bronx Zoo devised a search method for tigers, in which Cambodian staff set up automatic cameras along likely trails, to be triggered as animals crossed an infrared beam. Among several thousand recorded 'events' were many tigers, sufficient for a tiger expert at the Fund to suggest a Cambodian population of 700, which if true would make it 'the last, best Indochinese tiger population in the wild'. Heartening, but the exercise may also carry the seeds of the tigers' elimination, as it will increase the poaching effort. Indeed, a few of the remotely shot pictures captured poachers themselves. One more Cambodian treasure under threat.

At the Bayon, before climbing higher, I pause at one last mysterious creature, a giant fish chasing and about to eat a deer. Quite what the deer is doing in the water, or the fish on the land, is not clear, but the action is underscored by a short and roughly carved inscription, which translates as 'the deer is its food'. This is stating the obvious, but I defer as usual to Claude, who says that it is simply an instruction for the carver, intended to be removed later. The only really big fish in Cambodia is the giant Mekong catfish, an impressive creature certainly, but hardly equipped to consume deer. In any case, this is no catfish; the head looks more like a pit bull terrier. Perhaps this is some obscure political symbolism. There is a bas-relief from the same period at another temple that represents the perpetrators of an armed revolt as a giant monster, which a heroic prince overcomes in battle.

All these bas-reliefs surround the gallery walls at ground level. Within, the temple rises like a mountain, with small peaks at different heights, towards a central summit. The analogy is precise. State temples like this were actually models of the universe, the inner sanctuary located at the heart, under the summit of the world-mountain Meru, the home of the gods. We entered and started to climb. Just then there was the thud of an explosion, no echo, the sound flattened by the forest. Hard to tell how far away, perhaps a few hundred metres. I always took a keen interest in these distances.

The face-towers of the Bayon

'What was that?'

'I don't know.'

'Khon,' I insisted, 'can you find out?'

Later, in the evening, he supplied the story. Two soldiers had gone fishing, back in the forest of a city. The area is substantial, 900 hectares and an almost perfect square, its walls three kilometres a side. Almost nothing remains of the settlement away from the central area of the palace, royal plaza and State temples, but there are still ponds. It was to one of these that the soldiers had planned their outing, and the chosen method was a fragmentation grenade. I had seen this before, and it is very effective.

Although more expensive than fish bait, the pressure generated by an underwater explosion is intense. Fish in the immediate vicinity are blown to shreds, but many more for metres around are killed intact, ideal if you're planning a fish supper for a couple of dozen people. In this case, it had gone wrong. The grenade had been thrown, it fell into the shallow water but failed to detonate. Here logic failed to engage. What do you do with an unexploded grenade? Well, what you don't do is to give it another whirl. Yet that is what the soldier had attempted, wading in to retrieve it. Then it went off, killing him outright.

STONE FACES

We emerged through the warren of interior steps and corridors on to the terrace that surrounds the central circular massif of the Bayon. Even reconstructed the temple is convoluted, having been through at least three changes of plan while it was being built between about 1200 and the end of the thirteenth century. When the French archaeologists first went to work, it was much worse. Henri Marchal, who took over as conservator in 1916, said:

I knew the Bayon myself when it was still submerged in a tangle of creepers and foliage. It was very impressive; . . . a fairytale, ghostly setting, but the architecture was totally destroyed. Nothing could be made out, neither the plan of the building nor its carved decoration; the significance of the bas-reliefs, invaluable documentation of the history of the Khmers, was completely lost. In a word, all scientific study was imposs-ible. Worse still, this green mantle, so romantic and picturesque, was itself a terrible agent of disintegration and ruin. Sections of wall crumbled, vaulted roofs collapsed and each year saw the disappearance of some fragment of this strange, majestic monument.

Here on the terrace, it is the face-towers that dominate. More than a hundred huge stone faces look down from different heights. Four to each tower, covering the cardinal directions, they have attracted endless hyperbole. At the time when Marchal first saw the Bayon, many were covered in vegetation, others were in pieces, which may explain why Henri Mouhot simply noted them without waxing ecstatic. Later visitors, however, more than made up for the omission. There was something peculiarly compelling about colossal stone effigies, unexplained and ruined, looking out over a decayed present. Piranesi would have had a field day here.

Giant stone faces surrounded by mystery, crumbled, encased in the roots of tropical trees, with enigmatic smiles – this is absolutely the stuff of romantic exploration. The poet Shelley did this kind of thing really well. Although not completely typical of the rest of his work, his late sonnet *Ozymandias*, written in 1817, is one of his best-known pieces. In it, he has a traveller 'from an antique land' tell the tale of discovering ruins in the desert. There is a giant statue, 'two vast and trunkless legs of stone', and close by a broken stone head. It is the expres-sion that Shelley concentrates on – and on what it reveals of the lost empire.

Half sunk, a shattered visage lies, whose frown,
And wrinkled lip, and sneer of cold command,
Tell that its sculptor well those passions read . . .

There is an inscription that identified the once-great ruler:

'My name is Ozymandias, king of kings:
Look on my works, ye Mighty, and despair!'
Nothing beside remains. Round the decay
of that colossal wreck, boundless and bare
The lone and level sands stretch far away.

Shelley had been inspired by a statue of Rameses II
(Ozymandias was a sloppy Greek translation of one of the
Egyptian ruler's several names), and was writing on one level
politically about the arrogance of power and its dissolution, but
also evocatively about the romance and mystery of ancient ruins.
For Rameses II substitute Jayavarman VII, replace the level sands
with jungle canopy, and you have the best epitaph of its kind for
Angkor.

Once Cambodia had been discovered by the West, who
visiting the Bayon could resist a literary excursion? Unfortunately, almost no one. The first writer to visit, in 1901, was
the French naval officer and exotic novelist Julien Viaud, who
wrote under the pen-name of Pierre Loti. A curious personality
who managed to combine flamboyance (his 30-room house in
Rochefort was a personal museum that included a medieval hall,
Renaissance, Turkish and Arabic rooms, a mosque and a
Japanese pagoda) with asceticism (he went on two Trappist
retreats), Loti was fulfilling a childhood ambition in visiting
Angkor.

At the age of fifteen he had come across a picture of the overgrown towers of Angkor Wat 'in I know not what colonial
review'. Since this was 1865, it could well have been an edition of
the *Tour du Monde* carrying Mouhot's account and published two
years earlier. For a boy who had decided on a life 'of travels and
adventures, with magnificent, even somewhat fabulous
moments, as for some oriental prince', this was a perfect goal.
Thirty-five years later he reached it, on a brief leave from his ship
moored in Saigon, and in a couple of days gathered enough
material for *A Pilgrimage to Angkor*, first published in 1912. Loti's

style is impressionistic and exotic – overblown and not at all to modern taste. In his day, however, he had a reasonable literary reputation in France, and became the youngest member of the Académie Française.

Loti gives it his all. 'I shudder suddenly with an indefinable fear as I perceive, falling upon me from above, a huge, fixed smile; and then another smile again, beyond, on another stretch of wall; then three, then five, then ten.' Loti has indeed fallen under the spell of the face-towers of Angkor, their magical ability to evoke silly thoughts. 'They smile under their great flat noses, and half close their eyelids, with an indescribable air of senile femininity, looking like aged, discreetly cunning old ladies.'

Pierre Loti set the precedent, not badly written for awe-struck pondering, but it all goes downhill from here. Others followed, many less talented, and as Angkor found itself on the Asian grand tour in the 1920s and '30s, amateur travellers tried their hand. Perhaps the nadir of gush was reached by one P. Jeannerat de Beerski, who wrote in the 1920s:

> One finds at one time that he has the disturbing sneer of sadism, at another the chilling disdain of overwhelming superiority, or else the annoying hypocrisy of absolute egotism. Always, however, pure goodness is non-existent, and one feels that his ideas can only range between controlled wildness and unlimited culture of evil.

Shuddering at this, he frets: 'Shall I walk for ever, always in the Bayon, till I fall of exhaustion? . . . Shall I die, lost here?'

Or perhaps it was the breathless H. Churchill Candee: ' . . . an entrancing mystery deep in the jungle, soft and alluring in the twilight made by heavy verdure, accessible only to the ardent lover of past days who is gifted with agility.' Little wonder that she '. . . stands before it stunned'. The reader too.

I'm indebted to Dawn Rooney for unearthing these, although I think they would have been better off left buried. Even Somerset Maugham, who should have known better, succumbed to the urge in *The Gentleman in the Parlour*:

. . . heavy, impassive faces loom out at you from the rugged stone. Then they are all around you. They face you, they are at your side, they are behind you, and you are watched by a thousand unseeing eyes. They seem to look at you from the remote distance of primeval time and all about you the jungle grows fiercely. You cannot wonder that the peasants when they pass should break into loud song in order to frighten away the spirits; for towards evening the silence is unearthly and the effect of all those serene yet malevolent faces is eerie.

After all this, what do I think when I see them for the first time? Knowing the efforts of Loti, Maugham *et al.*, I'm far too cautious to add any more purple prose. Besides, I'm a little stoned, because Roger has brought some of the large parcel of ganja that the *cyclo* driver delivered to the government guest-house in Phnom Penh. It's the end of the day, and with local rum poured into some freshly cut green coconuts, we are having drinks on the terrace, accompanied by a joint. In the absence of cigarette papers, this is rolled in a 50-riel note (1979 variety) bearing the image of one of these face-towers, and although this does nothing for the flavour, being an old note that has spent too long in sweaty tropical back pockets, the idea seems to me poetic.

What I do find impressive is the balance of sculpture and architecture. The entire upper level of the Bayon is an inter-locking set of massive sculptures, and at the same time a temple building. The art is structural, and the structure art. There is nothing else quite like this in the world. There have been other colossi, but none worked into the fabric of the building. Greek caryatids have some similarities – both sculpture and column – but they are very much a part of the architecture, and on nothing like this scale.

As for the expression on the faces, they might benefit from less attempted explanation, given that this is inevitably a fruitless exercise. A considerable amount is known about the Bayon – more than most casual visitors realize – including that it was the site for worship of different cults and religions, separately and concurrently. These include the Pantheon of Gods, Hinduism and Buddhism. To have some opinion about the expression (compassionate, condescending, sneering, whatever), it would help to know which divinity the faces represent; indeed, why they are here at all.

An early candidate, reasonably enough, was Brahma of the Hindu Trinity. Reasonable because one of the distinguishing features of this god is his four-faced head. Not conclusive, but a good start. Then Parmentier in 1924 discovered a pediment clearly showing Lokesvara, the compassionate Bodhisattva – a Buddha-to-be, who had achieved Enlightenment but remained on earth to help mankind. This shifted opinion towards a Buddhist representation.

Perhaps it's as well just to settle for counting them. This should be simple enough, but there is still disagreement about the number of towers, due to rebuilding, additions and collapse. According to one view, there were 49 originally, although the French scholar Paul Mus believed that there should have been 54. There are 37 still standing, and not all have their full complement of four faces. This was too much of a headache at the end of a long day, and we gave up counting. As we drove back to town at sunset, the duck hunter was still popping away and the ducks were still flying. Perhaps the plan was to keep them in the air until they dropped from exhaustion.

PRESERVATION AND EXPLOITATION

Ruins are what most visitors to Angkor want to see. Big is good, but desolate is better, and in the Angkor Business, presided over for a century by archaeologists and historians, this generated a conflict of interest. As an archaeologist, you make your name by restoring a monument, and generally speaking there are not enough of these in the world to go round. Rather like tribes for anthropologists. Angkorean temples are among the last available, and almost everyone is bidding for them. Under the aegis of the École, the French, more or less by historical right, have the largest project – the complete restoration of Bapuon. This massive, ruined pyramid was for at least 300 years one of the

Strangler fig encasing an entrance, Ta Prohm

One of the gods pulling the serpent Vasuki, the Churning of the Ocean of Milk,
North Gate of Angkor Thom

most imposing temples at Angkor. Built in 1060, it was surpassed by Suryavarman II's Angkor Wat in the mid-twelfth century, but even at the end of the thirteenth century it still dominated the city of Angkor Thom. Zhou Daguan described it as 'the Tower of Bronze, higher even than the Golden Tower [Bayon]: a truly astonishing spectacle, with more than ten chambers at its base.'

But by the time the French arrived, it was hardly recognizable as a man-made structure. The task of restoring it was so great that it had hardly begun by the time that the Vietnam War spilled over into Cambodia and reached Angkor. Bernard-Philippe Groslier, conservator at the time, conceived a heroic plan. The outer cladding of sandstone would be removed and a new structure cast in concrete. He had barely started when the Vietnamese moved in, in 1970. He was allowed to work for a while, crossing the front line daily on his bicycle, but eventually had to leave. He died in 1986, but now the EFEO is back, on the largest of Angkor's many restoration projects. Work is under way almost everywhere.

Angkor's popular appeal is firmly rooted in the adventure of lost ruins, but of course this is largely despised by the professionals, who want to get on and *do* something. Nevertheless, the French took a decision that was resoundingly successful with visitors – to preserve one temple in a manicured state of abandon. They chose Ta Prohm, one of several late twelfth-century temples. They made it structurally sound with the judicious insertion of concrete beams and pillars here and there, but none of them obvious. They kept it weeded, but left the giant trees. Two species in particular have grown in and around the stones to the extent that they are now an intertwined part of the monument. The larger is the silk-cotton tree (*Ceiba pentandra*), with enormous pale-brown roots that some of the sailors in the French expedition of Louis Delaporte in 1868 first took for serpents. The smaller is the strangler fig (*Ficus religiosa*). In both cases, the trees began life from seeds dropped by birds on towers and gallery roofs. Then, as Pierre Loti wrote,

. . . no sooner did it germinate than its roots crept like tenuous filaments, insinuated their way between the stones, to go down, down, guided by a sure instinct, towards the earth. And when at last they reached the earth, they quickly swelled, waxing on its nourishing juices, until they became enormous, disjoining, displacing everything, splitting the thick walls from top to bottom.

They have, in fact, become the armature of the ruin, first having forced the stones apart, now holding them together. All the visitors love them.

In fact, a temple that is fully overgrown, has never been *dégagé*, is unintelligible. I once rooted around a smaller temple, Ta Nei, while it was still shrouded in a thicket of undergrowth. The walls were invisible until I found myself within a few metres of them. André Malraux described his encounter with Banteay Srei as it was in 1923, only nine years after it had been discovered by a Lieutenant Marec. One of the party points 'towards a dark mass whence canes were sprouting here and there, half-hidden in the forest . . . they came upon a clump of cane-brake, interlaced like wattles, which, rising to a man's height, formed a natural palisade between the ruins and the forest'. This is the outer wall, overgrown and stippled with moss.

The year 1989 was a good one for overgrown. The temples had been left to their own devices for two decades, and the dipterocarp forest, nourished by Cambodia's monsoons, had gone back to work unhindered. In fact, the really impressive encroachment and dismemberment of the monuments by trees take many decades, but even in twenty years there had been a healthy crop of grasses, creepers and bushes. One morning we entered Preah Khan, another of Jayavarman vii's temple-cities, from the west, the only practical approach at that time. Every evening I passed on our itinerary for the next day as a request to the Governor's office. They notified security, and armed guards met us at agreed times at temple entrances, usually before dawn.

On this day, there was no one. We waited, I as usual impatient to get started. Ten minutes passed, still no guards, and I could already see, high in the canopy, the first sunlight catching the treetops. Time to start photographing. I couldn't stand it any

Sweeping the manicured, controlled decay at Ta Prohm

Silk-cotton trees invade a gallery at Ta Prohm

longer, and set off with the cameras. The approach to Preah Khan, which was more than just a temple – a Buddhist university with more than 1,000 teachers and supporting city, with 97,840 people producing ten tonnes of rice daily – was broad and magnificent as built, a 150-metre causeway lined with stone pillars, after which came giant statues of gods and demons holding the bodies of enormous serpents. None of this was visible. Instead, there was a meandering trail through chest-high grass, and we followed this in single file, the others following me.

There was a shout from behind, something I couldn't make out in Khmer, followed by Khon yelling at me to stop. I turned. One of our newly arrived guards was trotting towards us. He pushed past me and slowed to a walk until he reached a low bush about 10 metres ahead. He knelt down, there was some rustling of grass, but I couldn't make out what he was doing. The bush moved a little. After a minute he stood up and beckoned us on. When I reached him I paused to look down. There was a rocket-propelled grenade lying on the ground. It had been lodged low in the bush, and the guard was now neatly coiling up the wire that had been stretched across the path. Yet another use for grenades.

'I told you to wait, but you wouldn't listen', Khon said reprovingly. There was no argument to that.

I said: 'In future, Khon, let's have a new system. Guide goes first.' He giggled.

All this high-octane romance is coming to an end. In destination tourism, clients want the evocative, magical experience on schedule and in comfort. The industry is only too happy to provide, with flights and hotel rooms. As many as you like. Fly them in, scoot them round the temples, fly them out. On average visitors spend three days at Angkor, by which time they have seen enough ancient monuments to last them at least a year and are ready to head back to Thailand, Singapore and Vietnam for beaches, swimming pools and spas. And the international tourist industry is nothing if not efficient. In 1987 there were just 440 visitors, but once the peace issue had been settled in the late 1990s the numbers began ramping up: 60,000 in 1999, a quarter of a million in 2001. The only uncertainty is exactly which year in the next two or three will see the magic threshold of one million crossed. Angkor is big business.

The only problem with this neat solution to Cambodia's economic woes is that the tourism can deliver only on amenities. On the experience it actually has a destructive effect. What none of the tour companies likes to remind people of is that, with hundreds of people crowded at the western gate of Angkor Wat to watch the famous sunrise over the towers, the atmosphere is somewhat less than sublime. And Henri Mouhot's solitude as he sat on top of Bakheng hill looking out over the monuments has been replaced by a horde of panting, sweating tourists who hike up (or, if flush and lazy, ride on an elephant) to jostle for a view of the sunset. Oddly, on these occasions – and Angkor is only one of many destinations with a celebrated sunset view – most of the spectators crowd on the west side to watch the sun go down, rather than on the east, from where the view of Angkor Wat is magnificent.

So what to do about this dilemma? The partly overgrown temples are wonderful if you come across them on your own and in silence. That's the way they're marketed. And the more that tourists are drawn to this elusive experience, the more it slips from their grasp.

The issue has certainly exercised the Cambodian government, but the conflict between conserving and exploiting has only increased. The development plans have been quite forth-right, and have included a mobile sound-and-light show roaming from temple to temple, the world's largest balloon tethered close to Angkor Wat, handing everything over to a Chinese Malaysian contractor to run on efficient Disney-like lines, and installing an escalator on Bakheng hill. So far just the balloon has appeared, a huge yellow helium-filled sphere that goes up and down every ten minutes like an elevator. A million-dollar investment, it might have difficulty paying for its keep; a professional balloonist I met later in Bagan was adamant that no commercially operated tethered balloon has ever been profitable.

And Angkor Wat did experiment with sound and light, after a fashion. In December 2002 José Carreras sang to an audience of 1,000, with dinner thrown in. The event was staged by Raffles, the current owners of the old Grand Hotel, and was a sell-out, even with the tickets priced at US $500, $1,000 and $1,500. The chairs had to be trucked in from Thailand (there were not that many spare in Siem Reap) and the accommodation problem – of there not being 1,000 five-star beds in town – was solved by striking a deal with the Oriental in Bangkok. The Oriental chartered aircraft to fly guests in for the show, and back to Bangkok at the end of the evening.

Ranged against such imaginative schemes are the conservation professionals, chiefly in the form of the Cambodian authority created to look after the monuments and called APSARA. Even the commercially minded members of the government appreciated the need for something like this, because of the stringent conditions laid down by UNESCO for any location that wants to become a World Heritage Site. This label is very good for business, rather like an ISO approval rating. APSARA's problems, however, have included inexperience, nepotism, infighting and hints of corruption. Most of its solutions have been schoolmasterly, restricting access, roping off sanctuaries (including the entire inner enclosure of Banteay Srei) and generally telling people not to do this or that. One of its more heroic plans was to ban all motorized traffic from Angkor, replacing it with electric buggies. Perhaps not that bad an idea, provided that no one in authority was found to have a business interest in said buggies. Hun Sen has made no secret of being opposed to this kind of APSARA initiative. 'I don't know where these people come from who write such measures', he said. 'Maybe they should develop the moon, which is uninhabited.' It's payback time at Angkor. For Chenla the Rich, Angkor the Great has become Goose the Golden.

III Tomb Raiders: Looting and Faking Khmer Art

Shortly before Christmas 1923, André Malraux stood in the tiny enclosure of Banteay Srei, Angkor's most exquisite temple. His career as writer, philosopher and eventually minister of cultural affairs in General de Gaulle's government lay ahead. Literature, in which he would become an iconic figure of the Left, was not on his mind at that moment. The purpose of his visit, conceived in Paris some months earlier, was to steal sculptures.

Malraux was up-to-date with the contemporary market in art and antiquities, and it was to this world that he turned when he discovered that he was ruined. Married at 21 to Clara Goldschmidt, he had shortly afterwards invested a large amount of his wife's inheritance in highly speculative Mexican mining stock. A year later the mining company collapsed and they lost everything. Malraux's solution was characteristic of his view of life – instead of pulling in his horns and accepting a bail-out from his father-in-law, he decided to be bold. An audacious plan was what he needed, something that would solve the problem at a stroke, preferably with an element of adventure. He quickly found it in Cambodia.

The basic scheme was to find an undiscovered, unlooted Khmer temple and . . . well, loot it. He would simply 'take some statues and sell them in America'. His inspiration was the notion of the Royal Way. As Malraux explained it, the ancient Khmers had built a network of die-straight highways linking the capital Angkor to the provinces, and at intervals along these roads were temples, in much the same way as the road through France 'was staked out with cathedrals, sanctuaries, and small chapels, just like centuries later the Spaniards in California set out the route along the Pacific Coast by missions, one day's ride from each other'.

94

The inner enclosure of Banteay Srei

In reality, lost and ruined temples are indeed linked by this road – or rather roads, for there were at least four, spreading out from the capital. Little remains, except for a few stone bridges and some curious chapels known as 'Houses of Fire'. According to an inscription at the temple of Preah Khan, there were 121 'Houses of Fire' placed at regular intervals along the roads – long stone halls with a tower at one end and windows along one side. The ceremony performed in them is unknown, but they may have been used as staging posts for armies on the march. Those that have been found mark the existence of the road.

The Royal Way enjoys the mystery of never having been fully explored and having, for the most part, disappeared. Malraux saw its romantic possibilities, which because of modern Cambodia's disastrous history are no less today. Although Banteay Srei is now well within the tourist circuit of Angkor, this is a very recent thing. On my first visit to Angkor in 1989, no inducement would persuade the army to escort me there, even in an armoured troop carrier – they had just lost some men to a Khmer Rouge rocket attack on the road. The little temple was a surprisingly late discovery at Angkor. Although only 20 kilometres north of the main complex of temples at Angkor, it had escaped even the thoroughness of Lunet de Lajonquière's survey of Khmer temples from Siam to Cambodia. Given its popularity with tourists now, this might seem surprising, but the forest was relentless in its recovery of temples. After all, in the hills a few kilometres north of here is another well-visited site on the modern itinerary, the River of a Thousand Lingas, with carvings of *lingas* and Hindu gods in the stone of the stream-bed, and this was discovered only in 1968. It was an official in the Geographical Service, a Lieutenant Marec, who came across Banteay Srei by chance in 1914.

This made it ideal for Malraux's purposes. It was not actually on a Royal Way, but never mind. It was unrestored and had some of the finest carvings at Angkor, in deep relief in a pinkish-red sandstone from local quarries. In October 1923 he and Clara set sail on the auspiciously named SS *Angkor* from Marseilles. In Saigon they met up with his old schoolfriend Louis Chevasson, whom Clara called 'the colourless one', and the three sailed up to Phnom Penh, then transferring to a riverboat up the Tonlé Sap to Siem Reap. They took horses and guides and rode north.

The trek up the lost road appealed to Malraux's sense of adventure. Arriving at the temple, he organized local help to lift and crate the seven stones that made up the relief of sculpted goddesses. As he later wrote in *La Voie royale* (1930, 'The Royal Way')

> Before him lay a chaos of fallen stones, some of them lying flat, but most of them upended; it looked like a mason's yard invaded by the jungle. Here were lengths of wall in slabs of purple sandstone, some carved and others plain, all plumed with pendent ferns. Some bore a red patina, the aftermath of fire. Facing him he saw some bas-reliefs of the best period, marked by Indian influences – he was now close up to them – but very beautiful work; they were grouped around an old shrine, half-hidden now behind a breastwork of fallen stones. It cost him an effort to take his eyes off them. Beyond the bas-reliefs were the remains of three towers razed to within six feet of the ground.

Clara wrote:

> We weren't the first to behold it, but we were no doubt the first to see it like this, to have our breath taken away by the grace of its stateliness, by its beauty, superior to any of the temples we had seen so far, all the more moving because forsaken. Seeing only the pink rock face, I moved forward when my eyes caught an emerald snake curled up at my feet [no doubt the highly venomous Hanuman snake]. It formed a gleaming hoop larger than a car wheel. Warned by our presence, it reared its head, which was as elegant as the temple, then slipped away among the stones that might conceal a sculpture fragment. That's how I found myself in Banteay Srei.

With crowbars, a hoist and ropes they slowly removed the blocks that made up each relief of a *devata*, but the men from the local village were increasingly sullen and moody. Malraux obviously was not aware of the tale of King Mongkut's attempt to remove the towers of Ta Prohm. Instead, it seemed to him, with remarkable naivety, that no one would either care or notice that he was removing the temple's most beautiful sculptures. For all Malraux's enlightened, liberal views and anti-colonial stance, he could not shake off the idea that because this was, for him, the ends of the earth, he could simply waltz through Cambodia and do as he pleased.

George Groslier, founder and director of the École des Arts Cambodgiens, had other ideas, and played a major part in their arrest. Of course, their activities had not gone unnoticed, and although Malraux, Chevasson and Clara succeeded in getting the 600 kilograms of packed stones back to Siem Reap by ox carts and then to Phnom Penh by riverboat, they were promptly arrested on arrival in the city. It was only through Clara's efforts, organizing a petition among the leading artists and writers of Paris, that they escaped imprisonment.

Both Malraux and Banteay Srei survived the botched robbery and went on to greater things. Malraux became the leading French novelist of the Left, and eventually France's first minister of cultural affairs under de Gaulle. Banteay Srei became the first Khmer temple to be reconstructed by anastylosis, the technique invented by the Dutch to rebuild Borobudur in central Java. Anastylosis was essentially a 'pure' method of rebuilding, using the original materials and construction methods appropriate to the particular temple. It was exactly this pillaging that elevated Banteay Srei to a high priority in the programme of restoration. On Malraux's arrest there was an immediate judicial order requiring a detailed study of the damage, and Henri Parmentier, the EFEO head of archaeology who had so enthusiastically endorsed Malraux's visit a month earlier, began this immediately.

Ironically, Malraux made full use of his experience in his literary career, turning it into the core of his novel *La Voie royale*,

One of Malraux's objects of desire: a *devata* at Banteay Srei

the second of his three Asian books. On the surface an adventure in the tradition of Rudyard Kipling's *The Man Who Would be King*, it was also an exploration of men's destinies and the need to define their humanity by action – something that Malraux returned to in the novel that established his reputation, *La Condition humaine* (1933, 'Man's Fate'). In *La Voie royale*, the hero, Claude, has exactly the same plan as did the author, exploring the Khmer Royal Road to find a lost temple and rob it, engaging the help of an older adventurer, Perken.

Possibly chastened by his three-year suspended jail sentence, Malraux developed his ideas about collecting antiquities in a different, more intellectual direction, and in 1947 published his solution to the many problems inherent in works of art in his book *Le Musée imaginaire*. Malraux's argument ran that a notional museum could be personally constructed in the memory, aided by photography. Instead of a limited physical collection in a fixed location, you could collect anything you liked and, as a creative curator, make new associations between pieces.

Such a non-invasive plan was certainly in stark contrast to his first excursion into the world of art history. Was this a reformed view from a Malraux who had learned his lesson, or more subtle apologia, contending that art belonged to everyone and that sacred objects somehow gained by being liberated from their original settings? With Malraux it was hard to tell. At the heart of *Le Musée imaginaire*, however, was the argument that, by taking a religious icon from its original setting, it was released from the slavery of functionalism. By a form of 'metamorphosis', he insisted, the object loses its original divinity but becomes resurrected as a work of art. As well he might.

In August 1966 Cambodia was preparing for the visit of General de Gaulle. By this time, Malraux had been appointed minister of cultural affairs, and was looking forward to returning to Angkor. But the new conservator was Bernard-Philippe Groslier, the son of the man who had insisted on Malraux's arrest in 1924. Groslier let it be known that if Malraux accompanied the President, *he* would be on holiday and so unfortunately unable to show anyone around. Malraux stayed behind.

Looting Cambodia has a long tradition, beginning with the spoils of war. Invasion and conquest throughout the region were always followed by a comprehensive sacking, and most things that could be moved, including whole populations, were carted off by the victor. As Angkor's neighbours grew more belligerent and more powerful, it came under more frequent attack. Following its greatest defeat by the Siamese in 1431, the capital was stripped. Among the treasures taken were large numbers of bronze statues, which were removed to Ayutthaya. This, however, was not the end of their journey. In the wars between Siam and Burma, King Bayinnaung, a Taungoo ruler who managed to unite the Burmese for a while, took Ayutthaya in 1564. The bronzes were removed to Pegu. A century later, in 1663, another Burmese king, Razagyi from Rakhaing in the west, seized them. Finally, six figures, including two of Shiva, one of the three-headed elephant Airavata and three lions, ended up in Mandalay, where they are now worshipped in the Mahamuni Pagoda. Their patchy, discoloured appearance is due to the local belief that rubbing a part of the statue will cure illness in the corresponding part of one's own body.

Officially sanctioned looting also played its part, and in the case of Cambodia helped to found the great Musée Guimet in Paris. The inspiration for this came from the colonial competition between the British and the French. Having established a protectorate over Cambodia in 1864, the French mounted an expedition to the Mekong river, the prize being a trade route to China. It was led by the French representative in Cambodia, Doudart de Lagrée, in 1866, and among its many investigations were the ruins at Angkor. Inspired by this, one of its members, Louis Delaporte, returned in 1873 with his own expedition to collect the finest statues. These, in 1882, became the core of the collection of the Musée Indochinois de Trocadéro in Paris, and eventually, in 1927, of the Musée Guimet.

Nowadays, most of the smuggling takes place over the western border with Thailand. It is fairly easy to cross, and for the most part no one pays too much attention, unless fired up by special orders from above. The immediate destination for smaller pieces is the slew of antique shops in Bangkok. I wanted to see this low-level process for myself, and travelled with Danny first to Chanthaburi to visit Chai, the brother-in-law of a friend of mine and local businessman. He knew people in antiques in the border town of Aranyaprathet, and had some police connections that would circumvent the usual immigration procedures.

This border crossing is increasingly popular among Western travellers on a budget, but the advantages of cheap overland travel are mitigated by the experience of Cambodia's port of entry, the miserable, seedy little town of Paoy Pet. Thais have a different interest in it since the casinos have opened here. A prominent sign on the approach to Aranyaprathet from Bangkok, newly erected, gives a warning in Thai: 'Don't give your money to the Cambodian casinos.' On the reverse side is the shorter message, 'We told you so.'

We rode into Aranyaprathet in Chai's new, luxurious Mercedes, and headed for the crossing. Strictly speaking, Danny and I needed some documentation, but we were invisible behind the car's darkened windows, and Chai had a brief conversation with one of the Thai immigration officials. 'I told him I'd bring you back', he laughed.

Not that there was any risk of our staying. We made a quick tour around the scrappy market with its dusty lanes, enough to see that there was nothing of interest in antiques, although four fresh leopard skins pegged up in one stall would have excited any conservationist. We returned to Aran and started to do the rounds of the dealers. The general pattern was a paltry collection of odds and ends on display but, once Chai had asked for the owner and we had hung around long enough, increasingly valuable pieces would be brought out. Many bronzes. Costly, perhaps, but genuine? None of us was an expert. At one of the dealers, we achieved the next stage in the opening of the labyrinth – a visit to the back of the shop. In this case, it was a large shed, and in before us stretched a field of *lingas*, a couple of dozen stone phalluses sprouting from the concrete floor. Most were in the standard form of three different cross-sections encompassing the Hindu Trinity: square at the base, representing four-faced Brahma; an octagonal middle signifying Vishnu; and a round tip, incised with a stylized but recognizable prepuce, for Shiva. All had until recently been central images in ancient Khmer sanctuaries. Why so many, I asked? It seemed that they were not good sellers compared with figurative sculptures. A bit too minimalist, perhaps. The looters had misjudged the market or, more likely, they just took what they could and let the dealers worry about how to sell them.

For all Chai's talk of having friends in town, which he clearly did, we were not being very smart. After spending the afternoon driving around Aranyaprathet in the large silver Mercedes with its tinted windows, we had made ourselves very visible, as we were about to find out. It was almost a two-hour drive back to Chanthaburi, and we left rather late, at dusk. After twenty minutes we reached the military checkpoint and were a little surprised to be searched. Two soldiers rooted around in the back of the car with torches. It took no more than a few minutes, then we were on our way, driving fast along the newly surfaced road, hardly any other vehicles in sight.

By now it was dark and Chai was speeding. We hissed along in a tight pool of light. No signs of habitation, no traffic, just the tarmac and the branches of small shrubby trees lining the road. For some reason Chai had the headlights dipped, so that when it happened, it happened quickly.

We had a sudden glimpse of a motorbike, but right in the middle of the road, standing, no lights, a man holding it. Chai jerked the wheel to the left, but we hit the bike hard. The Mercedes, built like a tank, wasn't even deflected.

'What do I do?'

I said, 'Don't stop. Keep going.' Danny said, 'Well, I don't know . . .'

Complete blackness behind as we sped on. Something definitely wrong. There are two reasons for a motorbike to be standing in the middle of a border road in Thailand at night, and much the less likely is a breakdown.

'I think we just caught them setting it up . . .'. The procedure is: motorbike on road with rider attempting to fix it, car approaches, slows down to help, rider's accomplices emerge from bushes with weaponry, relieve passengers of valuables. Particularly if said valuables have been noted at previous check-point. In this case, however, Chai's reckless driving precluded the Good Samaritan performance that was expected.

Several kilometres further on we saw lights to the left, at a distance from the road. Chai turned into a narrow track leading towards a small building, drove some 50 metres and cut the lights and engine. This didn't leave us in too good a position if there was anyone really diligent behind, but was still better than doing the obvious and just driving on. The night was silent. After a few minutes a car passed along the highway at speed in the same direction that we had been travelling; then nothing.

We examined the damage. Expensive bodywork but nothing more serious. I discovered that the small bronze figurine in my case was missing, and for one unbalanced moment suggested returning. 'Michael, that's about the most stupid thing I've ever heard you say', said Danny. Chai started the engine, we turned in the narrow space and returned to the highway. Chai by this time was extremely nervous, counting the kilometres to Chanthaburi Province.

'That's my province', he said. 'I know the police there. We'll be all right. Do you think we'll be all right?' We were. Eventually, a sign flashed in the headlights, *Chiangwat Chanthaburi*, in Thai and English. Another hour and we were home.

But this was very small stuff. More dramatically, on the first night of one visit to Siem Reap, I woke at 1.20 in the morning to automatic gunfire and grenade explosions. In a multiple robbery and general mayhem, a number of unidentified assailants attacked the Angkor Conservancy. Blowing off the gate, and convincing the guards to run off with their display of firepower, they made off with several of the best pieces in one of the warehouses. For good measure they sprayed the UN compound with automatic fire and robbed two nearby houses. The toll: two dead, eleven injured (including one Portuguese tourist at the Grand Hotel who unwisely thought to look out of his window) and several (uncatalogued) sculptures. A later official government report that I saw predictably placed the blame on 'the Pol Pot Armies', but few people were in doubt that this was simply a well-executed robbery, probably with inside help. Years later I spoke to In Phally, who has been on the staff of the Conservancy since the 1980s. In fact, he grew up in the compound, where his father was buildings superintendent until killed by the Khmer Rouge when they took over the town in 1975. On this February night in 1993, Phally had returned home to sleep, although he often did a turn of duty during the night. This was lucky for him. The room at the Conservancy where he normally spent the night was sprayed with bullets. Indeed, one unarmed guard died. 'They knew exactly what they were looking for', Phally said. 'They went straight to that door.' He gestured to one of the buildings where the most important pieces were kept. 'They took only the best, so they must have had information from someone who worked here.'

In Phnom Penh a fortnight later, Pich Keo, the Director of the National Museum expressed his fears for the safety of even that collection. With Khmer art prices standing at more than £1 million for a top-quality life-size statue (as in a recent sale in London), there is every reason for renewed pillage. Khmer pieces appear with increasing frequency in Europe and America – and more than ever the best ones are likely to be sculptures of real importance. Typically, the pieces, in stone and in bronze, are unattributed. The dealers remain coy about the sources, not through ignorance but because they know that they have recently been plundered. Corruption is on the increase, and with the connivance of local officials it is becoming increasingly easy to remove large and important sculptures and transport them to Thailand.

But the principal artery of the Khmer empire ran north and west – Malraux's Royal Way – leaving the North Gate of Angkor Thom to link the capital with what is now Thailand, its destination Phimai. About 100 kilometres from Angkor it reaches Banteay Chhmar, Citadel of the Cat, the largest ancient city in the north-west of Cambodia, a tremendous complex inside a two by two-and-a-half kilometre city wall and moat. If Angkor itself was largely abandoned for 400 years, then this remote site was truly Cambodia's lost city. Even when building started in the late twelfth century, this was a dry wilderness, known as 'the sand country'. Contemporary with the Bayon, Ta Prohm and Preah Khan at Angkor, Banteay Chhmar has the same huge stone faces – King Jayavarman VII as the compassionate Bodhisattva – and a massive wall around the central complex carved with almost one kilometre of bas-reliefs.

After the capital moved from Angkor to Phnom Penh, the roads that fanned out to connect it to the outposts of empire had no use. There is no record of what happened at Banteay Chhmar, but it was in a war zone – the no man's land on the way to Siam – and was probably soon deserted. The grand Royal Ways withered to a scattering of trails leading from one occasional village to another. The city was forgotten by everyone except the farmers who used the inner moat to bathe their water buffaloes. Even in the twentieth century, the French did nothing with Banteay Chhmar. No restoration was undertaken, no excavation, not even clearing of the forest, which by this century had grown in and around the collapsing stone temple. Although one of the greatest of the French archaeologists, George Groslier, had a personal affection for the place, he did no more than look and make notes.

When the Vietnamese invasion succeeded in driving the genocidal Pol Pot from power at the beginning of 1979, the border areas became a new area of conflict. The Khmer Rouge occupied some, the KPNLF and Sihanoukists took control of others. Banteay Chhmar was close to a KPNLF stronghold and was spared major fighting. Also, unlike temples like Ta Muen Thom further north that were in the hands of the Khmer Rouge, there seems to have

Face-tower at Banteay Chhmar, 1993, before the serious looting began

been little if any theft at the time (at Ta Muen Thom, the Khmer Rouge used dynamite to break up buildings for the carvings).

The run-up to the elections of May 1993 gave a short window of opportunity to visit this remarkable site. I drove from Siem Reap with Janos Jelen, the UNTAC (United Nations Transitional Authority in Cambodia) Deputy Director of Civil Administration for the province – five hours in a tunnel of dust that hung in the air and coated the landscape on either side. By mid-afternoon the sun was shining a weak yellow through the haze. The tenuous control that UNTAC troops and civil police were supposed to be exercising was already dissolving. An hour and a half from Siem Reap we stopped at the village of Kralanh to see some of Janos's compatriots, Hungarians manning the police post. The room in which we were given coffee was lined with full rice sacks; at first glance I took them to be part of a food distribution programme, but was told they were hastily filled sandbags – the police station had come under fire two nights previously.

We drove on through Sisophon and Svay Chek, finally reaching the village of Thma Pok, a base for United Nations police and military observers. A major from Russian Military Intelligence met us at the police station where we were to spend the night, and escorted us from there. Mine clearance has hardly begun, the tactical map confirming what the abandoned land on either side of the road suggests (among the colour-coded pins on the map showing incidents there was a scattering of the dark-red ones for land mine injuries and deaths).

After 15 kilometres, the edge of a forest appeared directly ahead. A little closer and we could see water in front of the trees – the moat of the temple. We had already passed through the surrounding city limits without noticing them; after some 600 years there was little trace. The only settlement now was a small hamlet, named after the temple. It occurred to me that quite possibly the bamboo, thatch and wood houses might be the descendants of original dwellings. In the twelfth century, however, only Angkor Thom was larger.

The central sanctuary is one of the most complicated structures of any Khmer building, and unusual for being long and narrow.

The only practical way of moving around was at roof level, over the galleries and the remains of towers. In the late afternoon haze the features were not at first obvious, but as we crawled along a gallery roof the light caught a face carved on one of the towers, broad, fleshy lipped, with that famous enigmatic half-smile. There were others, draped with lianas or supporting trees.

We returned the following morning to see the temple's master-pieces – a series of eight multi-armed Lokesvaras carved on the west wall – only to find that this time we were not alone. There were voices from the other side of one of the galleries, speaking in Thai, which fortunately Danny and I could follow. One said: 'What do you think of this one?'; another replied: 'Sure, we can get that.' We made our way over, to find a group of young Thai men examining carvings on the lower walls of one of the towers, and taking photographs. We approached. Surprised, they told us they were soldiers from a unit across the border, on an outing. A Sunday cultural excursion for teenage Thai squaddies is such an original idea that even they sounded unconvinced as they told us. We volunteered that we were making a photographic record of the temple because of the threat of thefts. They nodded vigor-ously, agreeing that this was a serious problem, and we all climbed out of the ruins together, they to a capacious army truck, we to our white UNTAC four-wheel drive. On reflection, all we may have done was to speed up the process of theft. 'I suppose they'll just come back tonight for some of the pieces', Janos remarked as we drove away.

Our Russian major added that there was nothing that the UN could do about it. If their mandate left them helpless to stop the nightly political killings and occasional Khmer Rouge massacres of ethnic Vietnamese, art theft was a barely noticeable problem. The previous year, however, other forces appeared to have taken a hand. The major described what had happened. Eight men had been seen entering Banteay Chhmar one night, and the police were alerted. Relying on the moat to help seal the temple, the police surrounded the site, preferring not to enter and get involved in a fire fight. During the night, there was a muffled crash from inside, but no other movement.

When the police entered the next day, they discovered that a large section of gallery was freshly collapsed. The local UNTAC police also inspected the site, and concluded that the men had dug their own grave. In the process of levering out carved blocks, they had brought the many tonnes of gallery down on top of them. Still, the investigation was under local police control, and some aspects seemed a little strange. No attempt was made to recover the bodies, and the verdict rested on what the major called 'collateral evidence' – the circumstances and various tools and items of clothing left at the site. No one, however, seemed to have mentioned the smell, an unavoidable component in this climate. For the local Khmers, this was clearly revenge exacted by the tutelary spirit of the place.

Claude, who succeeded the great George Coedes as the epigrapher and historian of Angkor and the ancient Khmers, gave me a hard time about publishing the photographs from this trip. A friend and a collaborator on a number of books, Claude has long been very concerned about pillaging, and blamed me for giving this outstanding but remote temple publicity. Malraux's thesis that isolated temples along the Royal Way are good places to start building a private art collection still holds true. And I have to admit now that he had more than a point, as later events proved.

We met recently in Bangkok at a dinner party on the banks of the river, a warm, lush evening in the rainy season. The first thing he said, eyes glittering, was 'I have a scoop! A new inscription for Jayavarman VII from 1215.' Well, a specialized scoop, I suppose, but his far greater one was five years ago, and we talked about that. In December 1998, returning home to Paris from the opening of the Centre for Khmer Studies in Siem Reap, Claude changed flights in Bangkok. With time to kill before the night departure, he visited River City, a large shopping complex on the Chaophraya river known for its antique shops. Strolling around the upper floors, his eye was caught by a vertical slab of sandstone in one window. Looking closer, he was amazed. It was a door jamb from a Khmer temple, carrying an inscription. And he knew exactly where it was from – Banteay Chhmar. He recognized the inscription, because the last time he had seen it, and translated it, the door jamb had been in place at the temple.

This was an awful coincidence for the Thai dealer, the last thing he could have expected. Despite the fact that Thai script is partly derived from Khmer, and despite the use of Khmer words in sacred amulets in Thailand, it is illegible to almost all Thais, particularly since this was the thirteenth-century form. The inscription might as well have been in Martian. Thinking about it more clearly, as the dealer probably did the next day, putting this particular piece of Banteay Chhmar on public display was not a very clever thing to do – rather like offering for sale stolen silver with the owner's name engraved on it. Still, how could he have known that the one person in the world who could instantly identify it would walk by? These inscribed door jambs and *stele* are for Claude like old friends.

'I think he realized something was wrong', Claude told me, 'because he came hurrying over and said, "It's a replica."

"No it's not", I told him, "It's the real thing."'

Claude had very little time to do something about this; his Paris flight was leaving at midnight. He took a taxi up to Silapakorn University, opposite the Grand Palace, and explained the discovery to his contacts there. He asked if they could arrange an interview with the Director of the Fine Arts Department, which they quickly did. Claude went through the story again for the Director, who needed no persuading. 'I know you', he said. 'The inscription will be here within an hour.' And it was. The police raided the shop.

The alarm was raised. Finally, the Fine Arts Department was on the case. The tales of concerted pillaging at Banteay Chhmar were being taken seriously. Earlier that month, my friend Chris (he who had earlier attempted to enter the centre of the universe at Angkor Wat) visited Siem Reap, and Khon was eager to take him to Banteay Chhmar. 'It's only just been opened to the public', Khon said, 'You should go.' In town, Chris met Doug Preston, a writer for *National Geographic*, and his wife. Doug had mentioned that he was having difficulties with the story he had been assigned to. Its genesis had been a unique, ground-penetrating radar image of the entire Angkor site made by the Space Shuttle *Endeavour* in 1994. It had revealed a definite pattern of large rectangles northwest of Angkor Thom, very close but in an area that had not been thought to have ancient settlements or temples. The assumption was that there were undiscovered temple enclosures pre-dating most of the monuments. In the event, on the ground nothing much had been found. There were no hidden temples lurking beneath the soil waiting to be rebuilt.

Chris took pity on Doug and invited him to join the trip to Banteay Chhmar, which he knew from Danny and me was at least an evocative site in a wild state. They set off in two vehicles, Chris, Olivier (a French diplomat friend of ours), Doug and his wife, and Khon. When they arrived, after ten gruelling hours on the road, the group split up, Chris going around the long south wall heading west, the others taking the north wall. When he finally reached the western end of the temple, Chris was taken aback. There was a long breach in the west wall, and inside the enclosure was cutting equipment. This really did look like Malraux's 'mason's yard', with cut stones littering the ground and freshly painted outlines on some bas-reliefs, clearly indicating what was to be removed next. The others caught up with him. The work site was abandoned, or so it seemed at first. As they explored further, they heard voices from beyond one jumbled section of stone. At this point, Khon realized the danger they were in. This was a professional, large-scale operation. I read Doug's account in the *National Geographic* (in hero mode, he omitted the other members of the group apart from Khon, whom he referred to by his full name, Sokhon). It went:

> Sokhon picked a cut tendril. 'Look at this,' he said, his voice shaking. 'The leaves aren't even wilted. This is still going on *right now*. We've got to leave immediately.'

Then . . .

> Sokhon appeared with a look of sick fear on his face. 'There are fresh tire tracks back there, made by a military vehicle.'

And . . .

Sokhon came up beside me. 'Please,' he hissed. 'We *must* go.'

I said: 'Khon, somehow that doesn't sound like you. All that shaking, sick fear and hissing.' 'What did "hissed" mean?', he asked. 'I didn't get that one.' I explained, adding: 'was the writer just playing it up? Pumping the drama?' 'No, absolutely not', said Khon. 'I really was afraid, for two reasons. First, you know that there were still Khmer Rouge around then, and you remember what happened to the de-miner north of Angkor Thom.' This was a case in which a mine disposal expert working for the Mines Advisory Group (MAG) had been abducted, together with his guide, and taken to Anlong Veng, where they were murdered.

'Second', Khon continued, 'the hermit who lived there, the *rishi*, told me, "You're lucky you came today. If you'd been here yesterday you'd have seen them working day and night." And I knew the local military were involved. That was obvious. If we'd seen them, and they knew it, then something would have happened to us. Not there, because there's a village nearby, but on the road back where there's no-one.'

On Khon's instructions, they would not stop for anything, and in the darkness they deliberately ran two military checkpoints. The troops at each one were too surprised to react. At one a young Khmer soldier raised his rifle, but not quickly enough to use it. They sped on towards Sisophon. 'The two things I remember clearly about the journey', Chris told me, 'were first, that this was the one time in my life that I felt in danger of being killed, and second, the moonbow.'

'The what?' I asked.

'Oh, it's extremely rare. It's the night-time equivalent of a rainbow and you need very unusual conditions – a bright full moon on one side of the sky and falling rain on the other.' Chris takes a keen interest in meteorology, and somehow this excited him more than the very real prospect of being stopped by rogue elements of the Cambodian army. The next day they reached

Siem Reap, without mishap. The *National Geographic* story was saved; it had been an adventure.

Doug approached the authorities in Phnom Penh, and predictably nothing was done. In Cambodia, as in Thailand, the military have an extraordinary clout, and these were joint manoeuvres with a large financial stake. However, once Claude had raised the issue and the Thai government decided that this had all gone too far, things began to happen. There were tip-offs. In the following month, January 1999, the police stopped a ten-wheel truck of the kind used for transporting buffaloes. This was in the far east of the country, close to the Cambodian border, on the Suwannasri road between the towns of Sa Kaew and Prachinburi. In it they found 117 blocks of stone, numbered and in sacks. The driver told the police that he had collected the cargo at a dawn rendezvous with Cambodian soldiers. These stones, when assembled by the Thai Fine Arts Department, turned out to be two sections of wall from Banteay Chhmar, each carrying the bas-relief carving of a multi-armed Lokesvara.

A few weeks later Claude went to the temple to confirm the damage, and was shocked. In the west wall, which I had photographed exactly six years earlier, there was now a 36-foot-long breach. Where there had been eight Lokesvaras there were just two left standing. Another two were lying collapsed on the ground and the central four were gone. Some looting had been going on occasionally before, Claude knew, but nothing like this. 'I found that even in 1988 some artefacts were stolen, but this time it was made on a – if I may say so – industrial scale.'

Finally, in 2000 the Thais returned recovered Lokesvaras and the inscription to the National Museum in Phnom Penh. Bertrand Porte, the conservator, showed me the two sections of wall stacked at one side of the central courtyard, one of 63 blocks, the other 26.

'We'll have to find a better place to display them', he said, 'maybe even re-install them at the temple one day. Who knows?'

To reduce the weight of the pieces, each of the 89 blocks had been cut approximately in half, leaving the inner, uncarved part of the wall on the ground. Bertrand would have to go back at some point with a team and collect these discarded fragments.

'Look here', he pointed to a series of short, straight channels at the edge of one block, 'they used a pneumatic drill to split the rock. Well, it could have been worse.'

THE PHRA NARAI LINTEL

There had been one earlier high-profile theft of a Khmer carving, and its later recovery. This was the famous lintel of Prasat Phnom Rung, just across the border in Thailand, near the edge of the Dangreks. In 1960 restoration work was about to start at this important hill-top temple, a major reconstruction that was not completed until 1988. The lintel at the entrance to the central complex was a particularly fine relief of the god Vishnu reclining on a dragon-like serpent, floating in the Ocean of Milk, and in preparation for the rebuilding it was placed on the ground, like the other lintels.

It disappeared. There was no trail, at least none that the police followed. There were rumours, including a sighting of a US military helicopter, but nothing that could be substantiated. And that seemed to be that, until 1973, when Prince Subhadradis Diskul, a senior Khmer scholar, by chance visited an exhibition at the Art Institute of Chicago. And there the lintel was. This should have been a simple matter to deal with, but it had been acquired from the James Alsdorf collection and the museum stalled, believing it had acted legitimately. The Thais were furious, and the *Phra Narai* (the Thai name for Vishnu) soon became a national cause.

Thai pride can be persistent, and the call for the lintel's return was taken up across the country, more stridently as the years passed and the restoration of the temple neared completion. Even Thailand's leading pop group Carabao got in on the act with a hit record called *Thaplang* (Lintel). The disc's cover was a picture of the Statue of Liberty holding the stolen lintel, and the key line in the song went: 'Take back your Michael Jackson, just give us our Phra Narai!'

Still the Art Institute of Chicago refused to budge, on the grounds that 'Italy doesn't ask for the Mona Lisa back'. It was 1988 and Phnom Rung was almost ready to open after its lengthy

The lintel at Phnom Rung depicting a reclining Vishnu, after its return

restoration. At this point an American academic from Chicago, Allan Drebin, happened to be teaching a graduate course in Thailand and learned of the dispute. The museum's reaction affronted him. 'After seeing, I was outraged', he said, and on his return set about negotiating with the museum. By arranging for the Elizabeth F. Cheney Foundation, of which he was director, to donate the equivalent value to the museum, all the feathers were smoothed down, and within a few months the lintel was returned. The circumstances of the theft were never uncovered, although locals like to claim that all the people involved eventually suffered violent deaths.

FAKERS AND THIEVES

At the Phnom Penh museum, Bertrand Porte had been making some interesting discoveries. 'Come and look at this', he said, leading me through the workshop, where a team of Cambodians and a French internee were working on various artefacts with scalpels and other tools, to a storeroom behind. On a low wooden trolley stood a stone torso, its head lying by the side. These two pieces had been returned from the United States with some fanfare – another piece of Khmer patrimony restored. Except that something was odd about this supposedly eighth-century sculpture.

'The torso is good. No-one questioned its authenticity. But just look at the carving of the head.' I didn't need to be an expert (and I'm not) to see that the quality of the carving and the expression were both low grade.

'And the decoration of the chignon is all wrong. There's nothing like that from any period.'

Even so, it was with some nervousness that Bertrand recommended cutting into the head. These two pieces could have fetched in the order of US $100,000, and the operation would destroy that possibility. A band about a centimetre deep and five centimetres wide was removed from the right cheek around the side of the head, like a flap of skin. Indeed, it *was* skin of a kind, because although the core was rock, the exterior was mortar.

'This is about the best stone mortar I've ever seen', remarked Bertrand. 'They took finely ground sandstone, added an epoxy resin and some pigment. But look at that patina. It's wonderful. So subtle and natural.' Every expert who had examined the piece thought it was carved stone; instead, it had been moulded over a roughly hewn block.

'I'm still waiting for the analysis, but it looks as if they applied the patina *fresco*. And the mixture is extremely hard.'

Needless to say, the torso also was modelled in stone mortar. What Bertrand could not understand was how someone with the skill to create such a handsome torso, with the musculature and the slight stomach bulge so beautifully rendered, could also create such an incompetent head. If the fakers had simply not bothered to do a head, no one would have discovered the fraud. Stone is the ideal medium for this kind of deceit, because it is pointless trying to date it. All stone has its geological age, and that is that. A sandstone sculpture may have been made yesterday, but its material is still, say, 40 million years old. Only the subtleties of the surface treatment give it away: the trace of a modern tool, perhaps, or a stylistic mistake.

I was intrigued by who these fakers were. The looters and smugglers, of course, were criminals of one kind or another, with statues and lintels just a commodity, interchangeable with drugs, teak logs and arms, but the people who fashioned Khmer art anew definitely have skill. As I learned, it is a grey area. Representing the more acceptable face of faking was Yas. When I first met him, he worked at the back of a small shop in Bangkok's Soi 3, close to the Grace Hotel of dubious reputation. With permed hair, a gold earring and a rather studious manner, Yas was a highly talented sculptor, but unfortunately in a country that does not value original modern art highly. Craftsmanship yes, individual creative expression no.

With no formal training, Yas was an apprentice at a well-known antique shop, where he spent most of his time making stands and bases for ancient artefacts. Except that many were little older than his mounts. 'Dealers used to bring in all these fakes to be mounted', he recalled. 'They'd tell me they were real,

Yas carving a Khmer torso, Bangkok, 1982

but I thought I could make better ones.' In his spare time he practised, and soon discovered his talent. He studied Khmer art of the Angkorean period and, armed with all the references he could find, began producing exquisite copies of statues and fragments in stone. When I visited him he was squatting on the floor of the backyard chipping away at a torso in the style of the Bapuon, an art book next to it open at a photograph of a remarkably similar piece. Similar but not exact: Yas had the intelligence and skill to insert his pieces within the known body of work, not as direct imitations.

Had Yas lived and worked in the eleventh century, his sculptures would have been among the best of the period. Dr Piriya Krairiksh, one of Thailand's leading art historians, became familiar with his work and praised its excellence. 'Yas is not a slavish copier. He makes creative copies that are technically superb and capture the proper expression as well.' The problem is that his sculptures *are* among the best of the period, and are now distributed among museums and private collections around the world. Three of his heads have even graced the cover of *Arts of Asia*, a leading art magazine.

Yas claimed that he sold his Khmer sculptures as reproductions, but he was well aware of what happened to them. Indeed, he went to considerable trouble to make them appear authentic, including sometimes breaking off the head. He shipped the stone from the same geological formations in the Dangrek mountains from which the great temples were built (the abandoned quarries are still there). He had a chemical patina of his own invention. The final touch was for Thai dealers to take the pieces to the border area, from where they would re-emerge as having been looted from a Cambodian temple.

Now you could argue that people like Yas are protecting the real stuff by satisfying a part of the market. On the other hand, they may simply be keeping the market more active. Yas himself is clearly ambivalent on the matter. Possibly as a sop for his conscience, he has always 'signed' his pieces. His name in Thai script is short and decorative, and he works it into *every* sculpture in a hidden way. In some he has woven it into the complex chignon, in others on a tiny slip of paper, tightly rolled and inserted into a hole bored into the base – and then sealed.

But then there was Sunthorn, who certainly did not sign his pieces. In the flurry of activity that followed Claude's uncovering of the Banteay Chhmar thefts, promises of cooperation were made between the Cambodian and Thai armed forces and police. In Ayutthaya, the Thais raided the house and workshop of a well-known local sculptor and artist, the 62-year-old Sunthorn Sowapee. For many years he and his sons had been making reproductions, increasingly of Khmer pieces to supply the growing demand in the antique shops of the capital. Like Yas, his craftsmanship was exceptional. The head of the local Fine Arts Department office who led the raid said: 'He is one of the best stone-carvers in Thailand. Maybe there are three or four people who can do work like Sunthorn.'

But there was more at the house than just Sunthorn's handiwork. There were stolen originals, too, and when the police began dredging the ponds scattered around the property, and digging in the rice-fields, they found more than 500 ancient artefacts, many of them from Cambodia. One of the family's techniques was to take a real fragment and extend it, carving a new body, for example, to attach to a head. Over a period of 30 years, Sunthorn had built up such a position of authority and trust within this murky business that he was able to act as a middleman between the looters and the dealers. the police strongly suspected that at least some of the Banteay Chhmar hoard was on its way to him.

Ultimately, though, the problem lies back in Cambodia. The Thais are certainly predatory enough to take advantage of the situation, but the big thefts have the blessing of some powerful people. The vaunted cooperation between the armed forces of the two countries is marvellously hypocritical. Claude's efforts on behalf of UNESCO to get the authorities in Phnom Penh to step up the level of protection are seriously hampered by this. 'It's especially difficult', he said, 'as everybody knows that the Khmer army is doing or is involved in these thefts.' The new, safer route for smuggling is by sea to Singapore, from where artefacts can be shipped easily to Thailand or anywhere. Particularly laughable in the Cambodian–Thai accord of 1999 was the comment by the Thai Supreme Commander: 'There will be no joint naval patrols as the Cambodian navy is not yet ready.' No one is holding their breath.

The rewards are just too high, at least for the big boys. At the sharp end of the business, however, the men who do the hacking and the gouging see very little reward, if any at all. As the Banteay Chhmar investigation lumbered along, witnesses reported seeing a few hundred soldiers working with heavy machinery, and in a military operation like this, the state pays the wages. For the freelancers, things are hardly better. Roger and I visited the police station at Siem Reap to photograph some recovered heads of giant demons, stolen from one of the causeways at Angkor Thom. The local equivalent of the public prosecutor had decided that it would add to the occasion to parade some twenty convicts as well, all serving between six and ten years for robbing the temples. Shackled, they were led into the room containing the heads and made to squat in front of the stones. They had stood to gain the equivalent of about 10 US dollars for their work. It wasn't quite what I had expected for this photo opportunity, but I went ahead anyway, and squatted opposite the prisoners to photograph them. Their eyes were fixed on the floor ahead of them, expressionless, but I could imagine the humiliation and sensed the resentment. I finished photographing these grim-looking characters and we left the station. Roger muttered, 'I wouldn't like to be around here when they get out.'

Convicts with the heads of demons stolen from Angkor Thom

Revolutionary poster commemorating the tenth anniversary of the overthrow
of Pol Pot's regime

iv The Gall Harvest: The Road to the Killing Fields

It will take a very long time for the events of the 1970s to fade from Cambodia's memory. More than Cambodia's, for the Pol Pot years were so extreme that they imprinted themselves on the international consciousness. How this came about was a combination of circumstances. It helped that the run-up to this terrible period, with the American bombing, the savage battles in the rice-fields and the gradual encirclement of Phnom Penh, was among the last acts of the Vietnam War, which was more comprehensively covered by the news media than any previous conflict. It also helped that William Shawcross's attack on US involvement – and specifically on its architect Henry Kissinger – in the book *Sideshow* (1986), received such widespread publicity. It was the Vietnam War that had caught Cambodia in its net, despite the efforts of Norodom Sihanouk to keep the country neutral. Crowned in 1941, he had seen Cambodia through independence from the French in 1953, but also through a growing political conflict, with a right-wing congregating around him and a left-wing becoming more radical, more Communist and more in armed opposition – the 'Red Khmer', Khmer Rouge, as Sihanouk himself christened them. When the conflict in Vietnam spilled over into Cambodia, it triggered a civil war, with the Khmer Rouge pitched against the government. It also led to Sihanouk's overthrow by the ultra-nationalistic right-wing Lon Nol and others, and from the outset the new Khmer Republic was doomed in its conflict with both the Khmer Rouge and the North Vietnamese Army.

But in terms of awareness of what happened to Cambodia, perhaps most influential of all in terms of the audience it reached was the Oscar-winning film *The Killing Fields* (1984), which became for most Westerners their introduction to the country.

125

This, it has to be said, was a delayed publicity, and an awareness long after the event. As the war in Vietnam drew close to its inevitable end through 1974, the public and the media in America and Europe lost interest, and after the last flurry of news coverage as Saigon fell on 30 April 1975, that was it. Phnom Penh had also fallen, but with less publicity. The main event was over, and Cambodia and Laos did indeed appear to be side-shows that would quietly settle down. Or so it seemed to most Westerners, and in Laos that was largely true. But Cambodia sealed its borders and closed itself completely to the rest of the world.

It was, in any case, a number of years before the American public regained any appetite for the entire Vietnam episode. Unlike the Second World War, Vietnam did not immediately inspire film makers. The first major retrospective feature was *The Deer Hunter* by Michael Cimino in 1978, followed by *Apocalypse Now* by Francis Ford Coppola in 1979. Then *Platoon* by Oliver Stone in 1986. Stanley Kubrick, as usual taking longer than anyone else to gestate a project, released *Full Metal Jacket* in 1987. All were focused on Vietnam, where the US ground troops were (although the climax of *Apocalypse Now* was set in northeast Cambodia). The media's attention to what had happened in Cambodia came late, partly because the news was slow trickling out, partly because it was of marginal interest. Until the scale of the horror became known. As with the concentration camps in Nazi Germany, which were reported well before the Allied invasion in 1945, most people at first found it difficult to believe that the news from Democratic Kampuchea, as the new regime called the country, was not exaggeration. But the Cambodia-watchers in neighbouring Thailand were building up a disturbing picture from refugees arriving at the border – stories of forced labour, starvation, atrocities, death.

Practically every first-time visitor arrives with this background somewhere in mind, however vague the details. And sooner or later, one question rises above the others. How? How could such a thing happen here, of all places? The evident charms of the Khmers – their sense of humour, politeness, affability – the tranquil, timeless landscape of rice paddies, water buffalo, sugar palms, and the general hedonism of Southeast Asian tourism, all seem at odds with the terror and violence that took place. The more you know, the more dislocating the experience. You would have to be single-minded indeed, not to say unimaginative, to sit and watch Cambodian life pass by on a city street, or in a village shaded by palms and mangoes, and not wonder how these people managed to make a living hell out of their country, some of them doing, most of them done by.

There may not be a satisfactory answer, but at least part of the problem lies in the expectations of the onlooker. Take one well-known example, still very much in print. In 1950 the celebrated travel writer Norman Lewis visited Southeast Asia with some sense of urgency. The year before, China had closed its doors in the wake of the Communist victory, and it looked as if political changes were inevitable in Indochina. The result of Lewis's journey was the acclaimed book *A Dragon Apparent* (1982), which captured something of the strange transitional period prior to the Vietnam War. It included Cambodia, at that time very little known in the West. When the book was reprinted after the war and the overthrow of the Pol Pot regime, Lewis felt obliged to comment on the startling contrast between the Cambodia he had written about 30 years earlier (Siem Reap, for instance, was 'another slumbering Shangri-La') and the appalling brutality that followed.

Lewis's Cambodia had been extraordinary to Western eyes, a place where the devout allowed mosquitoes to feed on their blood, where passengers in taxis might find themselves offered a tip by the driver (surely even Lewis could not have thought this common), where life was torpid and above all Buddhist. Thus the Indochinese, being Buddhist, were 'therefore in essence gentle, tolerant, and addicted to pleasures and satisfactions of a discriminating kind'. What suffering could we have visited upon these sweet folk 'formed in the ambulatories of monasteries' to transform them into the terrible, implacable Khmer Rouge?

Possibly this is the wrong question. A sharper enquiry might be how and why so many Westerners persuaded themselves that Cambodia was a tropical Eden. I talked about this to Tim Carney, an old friend from the State Department who had served as ambassador in a couple of difficult countries and had been at the American Embassy in Phnom Penh until the final airlift from the football field. He remarked drily: 'Lewis confuses gentleness with politeness.'

But then Norman Lewis is only one of many travel writers who have persuaded themselves that certain undeveloped, exotic regions of the planet, standing in mysterious contrast with our own society, somehow hold the key to human behaviour. It's a sentimental, expectant view, and Lewis should have known better than to write such nonsense. Did he really think that the peasants who make up the bulk of the population had the time, resources, education or energy to be discriminating about refined pleasures, like so many mandarins and dreaming scholars?

The historian Michael Vickery paints a very different picture of rural Cambodia before the Vietnam War, in travelling through the northwest. Banteay Chhmar, the scene of our looting adventure, has attached to it a small village. This is part of the outer, less fertile rim of Cambodia, a region of drought, poor soils and malaria. The Khmers distinguish between *sruk*, civilized, and *prei*, wild, forested, untamed and uncouth, applying the distinction to people and behaviour as well the land. Here is definitely *prei*. Vickery was struck by the lack of hospitality, by the sullen independence of these people. They wanted nothing to do with officials and townspeople, who brought only trouble and demands. 'The villagers hated their pretensions and false promises of aid and development. Most of all they disliked the officials' wives, who minced about the footpaths in high heels with handkerchiefs held to their noses.'

Lewis also reported the prevailing French view at the time, shortly before independence, that the Khmers were simply not soldier material, despite all the evidence of history. General des Essars, the commander of French troops in the country, told him that he had 2,500 Cambodian troops under his command, and nothing would ever turn them into fighters. Their Buddhist religion, he told Lewis, had knocked all the aggression out of them. And Lewis believed this. Contrast this with the view of François

Bizot, who knew the Khmers considerably better, having lived in a small village, married a Cambodian, had studied local Buddhist practices in the years before 1975 – and had also been a prisoner of the Khmer Rouge, the only one ever released. 'Traditionally', he wrote, 'the Khmers have been warriors. At the time of French Indochina, the commando sections were composed entirely of these loyal, upright men, who never waver and are not afraid to die; they have an innate sense of the terrain and an instinct for camouflage and ambush', adding that the Americans via Lon Nol squandered this talent by attempting to turn them into GIs in a technological war, for which they were quite unsuited.

Nor do you have to look too far back before the Vietnam War to see the darker side of country life and all the potential for the savage treatment of political enemies. Michael Vickery recalls being told by a woman acquaintance how her father, a Battambang Issarak (independence movement) leader, 'used to keep his prisoners chained up beneath the house without food or water and then execute them on his own firing range a few hundred metres beyond the back yard. He was not a pathological sadist either, but a good family man remembered fondly by his widow and children.'

RITUALS OF VIOLENCE

There is, it has to be said, a vein of ferocity running through Khmer history. Yet it's not simple brutality but instead a rather strange, exotic variety. And the place where, for me, it begins is Angkor in the thirteenth century, in one of the more obscure accounts of the visiting Chinese diplomat Zhou Daguan. His entire account, *The Customs of Cambodia*, is endlessly quoted because, despite being short and in fragments, there is nothing from the Angkorean period to compare with it. I certainly haven't avoided quoting from it in this book, but the passage that intrigues me the most, and is elsewhere mentioned the least, is the tale of the gall harvest. Now, everyone seems to have an opinion on how many crops of rice Zhou Daguan was talking about, how people dressed and ate and lived, but this short, gruesome account seems to defy a full explanation, and so is generally avoided. It goes . . .

> Each year the king of Champa required a jar of human gall, containing thousands. At night, men were posted at many places in the cities and villages. When they met people out at night, they covered their head with a hood tied by a cord and with a little knife, removed their gall from the right side of the back. When they had a sufficient number, they offered it to the king of Champa. But they did not take the gall of Chinamen. That is because one year they mixed a Chinaman's gall with the others and all the gall in the jar rotted and they could not use it. Recently this usage has been abolished, but the functionary of the gall bladder still lives in the city, near the north gate.

I think we can discount the 'thousands' as an exaggeration. Well, I hope so, or it would really have been horrendous in a small medieval city. But even if it was just hundreds, this is still a remarkable event, and it's hard to imagine why anyone would leave their house on those presumably well-known nights 'in the eighth month'. The translation 'harvest' has a curious and unsavoury ring to it, echoing the modern term for acquiring body parts for transplant. Really, though, the gall harvesters were more like hunters, stalking and ambushing their victims by dead of night. What was going on here? Abbé Bouillevaux wrote that the custom still persisted when he visited Cambodia in 1850, although without going into details. And a memory of it lingers today in folklore. Khmer, so specific with its precise words for arcane things, has an exact description for this strangest of jobs. *Promat promang* is the gall hunter, invoked to scare children into good behaviour – the Cambodian bogeyman, on his way to get you. This is by no means as prosaic as the English translation suggests. *Promat* means gall, but *promang* is 'hunter' only in this context. There are no deer *promang*s or rabbit *promang*s, just gall *promang*s. In a culture with so little

130

recorded history, the language itself is often the evidence, even when, as here, it is opaque.

Now, strange though it may seem, bile of a different kind puts in an occasional appearance at the Southeast Asian table, in the countryside at least. Of the four Cambodian flavours, bitter is the rarest, and obviously rarer still in the cuisine of the West. And what more bitter than this dark-green liquid? Yet it has its role, a rather rough one, in Asia – a part of the forest, the hard peasant life, something unknown in the effete towns. It's also strangely addictive – a personal view, admittedly – and a taste that its devotees become rather proud of. In a perfectly ordinary, but good, little restaurant in Buriram, in the Khmer-speaking part of Thailand just north of the border, there was a small bowl of dark bile nestled among the regular table condiments. Water buffalo, I suppose (I didn't ask). When you buy meat in country markets around here, it's customary to pick up a small bag of the animal's bile at the same time.

But the human gall harvest had a ritual purpose, though exactly what can only be guessed at. What horrifies and trans-fixes about this centuries-old tale is the casual violence. With the hood and the rope, and the small slit with the knife, Zhou Daguan is writing almost as if the victim is expected to get up and stagger home, minus one organ. Hardly likely, but it adds to the surreal quality, and also to the underlying cruelty. Liver, gall bladder and bile are all part of the same system, and eating the liver of an enemy was, as Michael Vickery mentions, an old Khmer warrior tradition, because the gall that it produces is considered the essence of bravery. In line with other instances of cannibalism, this was ritual and connected with the idea of acquiring the energy, the spirit, of the slain. In particular, it was a custom of wartime.

Neil Davis, the Australian news cameraman who saw more combat in Cambodia between 1970 and 1975 than any other correspondent, came across it frequently, and estimated that one in five government troops practised it. 'It would generally occur after a very torrid, close battle', he told Tim Bowden, his biographer, with either hand-to-hand combat or within grenade-throwing distance of the Communists. In the heat of victory some soldiers would take out their knives and very expertly cut out the liver of one of their dead enemy. Sometimes they would eat a slice of it raw then and there, or they would take it back a few hundred metres behind the lines and cook it.

Occasionally the South Vietnamese would do the same, but by no means to the same extent, considering themselves more sophisticated than the Cambodians. The practice was certainly not considered unusual, and although it did not have a high priority in the aftermath of a battle, it was often spontaneous. Davis continued: 'If they had overrun a Communist position and killed their enemy at close quarters, they would eat the liver immediately. In those moments of high excitement they would hold it up to their mouths in the same way we might eat a hamburger.'

This, and other rituals of battle, victory and protection became a hallmark of the fighting in Cambodia in the 1970s. A friend of mine recounted watching troops heading out from Phnom Penh in the early morning as he had his coffee by the side of the road. By the beginning of 1975 the front line was a short drive from the city, and any kind of vehicle was pressed into service, including Coca-Cola trucks. At the end of the day, the same brightly painted red lorries trundled back down the boulevard, Khmer Rouge heads dangling from the side panels. In a culture that was, and is, in thrall to the supernatural, they had a talismanic role every bit as important as being a symbol of victory.

Talismans in general were in increased demand by the soldiers, and the most important were amulets – small icons, usually Buddhist images, hung around their necks. In close combat and moments of great tension, they would often put the amulet in their mouth and bite on it. Back in the nineteenth century, the Vietnamese emperor Minh Mang was exasperated by this Khmer belief in the magical power of amulets. All it did was to encourage revolt by boosting the confidence of Khmer fighters beyond common sense. In 1834 he took one of these 'sacred rocks', tied it around the neck of a duck, and shot the duck. The bird died, but without apparently diminishing the faith of the Khmers in their own amulets.

Some talismans were in the form of scarves, even shirts, on which were drawn complex geometric patterns enclosing letters derived from sacred Buddhist texts. These *yantra* take their power from the words of the doctrine, and are protective – of health, good fortune, prosperity and so on. Just the other day, the brother-in-law of a friend showed me a neatly folded US dollar bill that had been inscribed with one of these designs – this was for financial good fortune, and had been drawn by a monk. Variations on these *yantras* are also tattooed – on the chest, back, limbs, even the Adam's apple – and this is a tradition that had spread into Thailand. As with the scarves, different *yantras* protect against different misfortunes, and naturally, during the war, those magical images that would ward off bullets and violent death were the most in demand. Even more effective was to combine the kind of permanence afforded by a tattoo with the intrinsic protective properties of an amulet, and have a magical object embedded in the flesh. There was ample precedent for this. King Indravarman III, who took the throne in 1295 after he had deposed his father-in-law Jayavarman VIII, 'caused a splinter of sacred iron to be grafted into his own body, so that any thrust of spear or knife could do him no harm' (Zhou Daguan again). The new king, who had taken power just the year before the Chinese diplomat arrived, clearly felt the need for some supernatural armour, having lived through violent times and having instigated some his own.

THE SIEGE OF KOMPONG SEILA

At a late point in the war, ritual cannibalism gave way to a more practical and necessary kind in the notorious siege of Kompong Seila, a town 115 kilometres southwest of Phnom Penh between the wooded Elephant mountains and a smaller mountain range. From the beginning of 1974 the town was surrounded by Khmer Rouge forces, and completely cut off. The siege lasted nine months, during which the only means of supplying the garrison of a 1,000 Lon Nol troops and the 9,000 inhabitants were airdrops. Helicopters were unable to land because of anti-aircraft fire from Khmer Rouge positions in the hillsides overlooking the small valley.

Ten thousand people need many tonnes of food daily to survive, and even though the resilient inhabitants of Kompong Seila managed to grow rice and vegetables during this time – while they themselves were living in bunkers under the ground – it wasn't enough. The valley in which the town sat measured only one kilometre by a half, and artillery and mortar rounds were falling constantly from the hills – sometimes a dozen or so daily, once as many as 700, and on average around 300. Physical survival was the paramount priority, market gardening under shellfire difficult. The Lon Nol government, hardly efficient or focused in any case, could not keep up its airdrops, and the aircraft, compelled to fly high to avoid the ground-to-air fire from the Khmer Rouge, dropped about half of their payloads outside the perimeter. By September, four months into what was to become the longest military siege since the Second World War, the situation was desperate. Above all, what was lacking was protein. How the defenders hit upon the solution is anyone's guess, but it may well have been inspired by a familiarity with human livers, and the consumption thereof. But eating other people to survive was a world away from ritually absorbing the power of one's enemy. It was probably more different than any outsider would imagine, because Khmer fighters did not see the liver thing as cannibalism. Inevitably, mores gave way to pragmatism. It began with one dead Khmer Rouge soldier, killed near the perimeter during an attack. They pulled the body in and cooked it.

From that point on, cannibalism was formalized, and procedures were established for the provisioning. Just the garrison alone needed many bodies for the pot, so every night hunting parties were sent out, numbering between four and twenty men in a team. Routes were established out through their own minefields (even more difficult was dragging the harvested bodies back in). This was considerably more difficult than the usual night patrols, because they needed as many as possible, which made it important to kill silently. The toll reached as many as 30 in a night.

Neil Davis followed this story closely, and interviewed the hunters, and the cooks. They quickly learned how to butcher, and the prime cut was, as you might expect, the rump – the buttocks. Other possible steaks were the calves and the biceps. Fingers came to be considered a delicacy, some people liked the lungs, and brains too were eaten. Other parts of the head were not favoured, however, or the ribs, for some reason. Most of the body simply went into the pot, with whatever vegetables and chillies they had, to make what they called 'man soup' (*samlor sach manus*). Davis asked a group of soldiers who had been at Kompong Seila how this tasted. 'Quite nice', they replied. Davis probed: 'Well, what's nice then, like pork?'

'Oh', they said, 'better than pork!'

The siege of Kompong Seila was lifted by the Khmer Rouge in early March 1975, very shortly before the end of the war. The final battle was for Phnom Penh, and the troops were needed for that. The Lon Nol soldiers from the defending garrison moved to the capital, and fought on the front line there, about 25 kilometres from the city. 'Of course for them', said Davis, 'it was like a holiday by comparison', and they enjoyed it. These were by now very tough and quite strange troops. But the Khmer Rouge attacks in their sector soon dropped away, and they couldn't at first understand why. The reason, however, was plain. In this kind of fighting, with infantry in positions close to each other, both sides quickly learn whom they are facing, by trading insults and listening to the radio traffic. The Khmer Rouge soon knew that these were the hunters from Kompong Seila, and lost all enthusiasm.

There was a sequel to this story, almost at the end. Davis came across a Kompong Seila company well behind the front line, on strike because they hadn't been paid for months. The following day, he visited again, but found them unusually surly and withdrawn. Eventually, he was able to coax out of them what the matter now was. It turned out that the day before the paymaster had arrived, but without any money, Nevertheless, he ordered them back to the front. Their lieutenant refused until his men had been paid. At this challenge, the paymaster pulled out his pistol and ordered him again. The lieutenant repeated his refusal, and the paymaster shot him dead.

The men immediately avenged their lieutenant, who had been through the siege with them and was well liked. They killed the paymaster, took the liver, heart, lungs and biceps, and made their speciality soup. On his return to Phnom Penh, Davis sought out the general commanding this sector and told him that he had a serious problem on his hands. 'I said, "They've just eaten the paymaster." He didn't show any great surprise, and just said. "Heavens, I suppose we had better pay them then."'

This macabre tale gives an impression of the state of violent chaos into which the country had fallen over the five years of war. It began with the *coup d'état* in which Sihanouk was deposed in March 1970, while in France. He received cold comfort in the Soviet Union, but the Chinese welcomed him warmly, persuading him to head a resistance to the newly declared Lon Nol government. This meant an even closer relationship with North Vietnam, which already had some 40,000 troops stationed just within the eastern border. They quickly moved in to support their Communist comrades, the Khmer Rouge, and their most public action was to invade Siem Reap province and take over Angkor.

By 1973 the Communist forces had the upper hand and the war was on its way to being lost by the Lon Nol army, corrupt and inefficient as it was, despite the bravery of the individual soldiers on the ground. At this point there occurred the bizarre spectacle of a visit by Sihanouk and his wife Monique to occupied (or liberated, depending on your point of view) Cambodia. Together with one of the Khmer Rouge leaders Ieng Sary, they travelled from China down the Ho Chi Minh trail to Cambodia, where they were joined by the other two leaders of the revolution, Khieu Samphan and Saloth Sar, soon to become Pol Pot. Ridiculously clad in Khmer Rouge attire, including Chinese cap, *krama* and flip-flops, Sihanouk appears smiling in photographs, holding hands with his former enemies. For their part, the Khmer Rouge referred to Sihanouk with the old folk saying of using a 'water buffalo to get across the mud'. They were on their way to victory.

RETURN TO THE KILLING FIELDS

In 1984 *The Killing Fields* was released, and had a major impact on world opinion. Dramatizing the real story of the *New York Times* correspondent Sydney Schanberg and his assistant Dith Pran, it not only introduced the Pol Pot years to most of its international audience for the first time, it did so with great artistic success, gaining an Oscar for the supporting actor role. That it was both critically acclaimed and a commercial success brought the spotlight on to Cambodia in a way that nothing else could have. The British producer David Puttnam already enjoyed a strong creative reputation, most recently for *Chariots of Fire*, and assembled a talented crew and cast. Roland Joffe directed and Bruce Robinson wrote the script, together managing to avoid the structural difficulties with the story, not the least being that Schanberg effectively disappears from the scene for the last third of the film.

The real events unfolded against the backdrop of the last days of Phnom Penh. On 1 April Lon Nol fled the country, with a million dollars granted him by his government. On 12 April the last remaining US officials, including the ambassador John Gunther Dean, were evacuated by helicopter. Schanberg decided to stay on and cover the entry of the Khmer Rouge into the capital, which seemed less foolhardy at the time than it does with hindsight. Only a few people heeded the trickle of evidence that the Khmer Rouge had comprehensive and brutal plans for restructuring the entire society. Revenge was expected – the Khmer Rouge had already announced a list of traitorous enemies – but it was assumed that this would be limited. Dith wanted to stay and help his friend, and Schanberg did not dissuade him, a decision he soon came to regret. As the Communist troops entered the city on 17 April, the first shock

Haing Ngor at the Siem Reap killing fields, 1989

was their announcement that Phnom Penh must be evacuated, entirely and immediately. The reason given was to protect the civilian population from US bombing. People could take only what they could carry, on foot, and the command was enforced. Within days, Phnom Penh was a ghost town.

Schanberg's story, *The Death and Life of Dith Pran*, appeared in the *New York Times* magazine in January 1980 and it was this that caught David Puttnam's eye. He acquired the rights, and by early 1982 was making preparations for the production, including casting. A Cambodian doctor, Haing Ngor, was at the time helping refugees at the Chinatown Service Centre in Los Angeles. He had escaped from Cambodia at about the same time as Dith, in March 1979, fleeing towards the Thai border as the Vietnamese forces swept into his region. By coincidence, the film's casting director met Haing at a wedding reception. Casting him was brave – he had no experience as an actor – but Haing's volatile and passionate nature gave him a compelling screen presence. He already, like Dith, felt that he had a mission to expose what had happened to his country, and realized that few Americans had any idea. He was persuaded, and signed an acting contract.

I met Haing through a friend of mine, Roger Warner, who had co-written his autobiography, *A Cambodian Odyssey*. We all attended the wedding of another Cambodian, Samnang Siv, close to Roger's home in Ipswich, Massachusetts, in early 1989. Haing was a celebrity by this time, but intense and committed to achieving some kind of justice. We talked about visiting Cambodia, which was still occupied by Vietnamese troops. Pol Pot was still alive, and fighting continued in the northwest.

Haing's deep rage was fuelled not only by his knowledge of what had happened and of the suffering of so many of his countrymen, but by his own experiences. These had been every bit as harrowing as those of Dith, and in time forged a bond between the two men. Around midday on 17 April, both had been in hospitals in Phnom Penh, Dith with Schanberg at the Preah Ket Mealea Hospital, Haing performing an abdominal operation at the military hospital. Both came close to being executed that day.

Schanberg and Dith were with the British journalist Jon Swain, who described how they were dragged from their car by 'boys, some perhaps twelve years old, hardly taller than their tightly held AK47 rifles. Their ignorance and fanaticism made them super-deadly.' They were bundled into an armoured personnel carrier and driven about for half an hour. They were certain they were to be executed, but Dith saved them by persuading the Khmer Rouge that they were neutral journalists.

In Haing's case, Khmer Rouge soldiers burst in, one aiming his weapon at Haing's head, asking if he were the doctor. Haing had the presence of mind to say 'No, the doctor left a minute ago. You just missed him.' This scenario, the hunting down of educated professionals, was repeated across Cambodia in the following years, and both Dith and Haing learned to claim the same occupation, taxi driver. In some instances, even the wearing of spectacles was sufficient proof of being a member of the despised bourgeoisie, the city people, 'new people'.

Dith returned with Schanberg to the grounds of the French Embassy to the north of the city centre. This became the temporary sanctuary for approximately 1,000 foreign nationals and a similar number of their Cambodian dependants. Despite Schanberg's efforts to forge documentation for him, Dith eventually, on 20 April, had to leave with all the other Cambodians, on the orders of the Khmer Rouge, following the river of people who had headed out into the countryside. Something in the order of two million people were on the move that month, not just from the capital but from all the provincial towns, out to begin new lives as peasants – a plan already conceived by the secretive and as yet unknown 'revolutionary organization', *angkar padivat*. The leader, Saloth Sar, known by his adopted name Pol Pot, entered the city only after a few days, and secretly.

Saloth Sar and his companions had begun to form their revolutionary political views in Paris. After the assassination of his predecessor, Tou Samouth, in 1962, he became the leader of the clandestine Communists in Cambodia – clandestine because he and Ieng Sary and others of the inner circle never declared their party affiliations. In 1963, fearing that Sihanouk's police would learn that they were members of the party's Central Committee (there's no evidence that they were discovered), they left for the Vietnamese border, henceforth operating from the Cambodian countryside.

Haing had already fled Phnom Penh, and spent until the end of April looking for his fiancée, Chang My Huoy, whom he found. Like everyone else from the towns, they were assigned manual labour. First they worked in a quarry, later in the rice-fields, carrying earth for one of the Khmer Rouge's grandiose and ill-conceived irrigation projects, and repairing roads. The two million or so newcomers were billeted on villages, and how they fared varied widely, depending on the prosperity of the area, the attitude of the locals (who often, understandably, resented the intrusion into their lives) and the character of the Khmer Rouge cadre. Starvation was common. Much of the countryside could normally support itself, but with little surplus, and five years of war and the massively destructive American bombing had already reduced the land's capacity to produce food. Most of the refugee townspeople were, in addition, totally unsuited to this kind of existence.

Haing and Huoy declined physically. There was never enough to eat, and Haing was plagued with dysentery. Caught hiding arrowroot that he had found in the forest, Haing was tied to a tree and had the tip of one little finger chopped off by an irate young guard. When eventually he was accused of being a doctor by someone who had known him previously, he was tortured to admit it, but resisted. The final tragedy was that Huoy, pregnant, died when she went into premature labour, her only chance of survival a Caesarian section that Haing, without surgical instruments and drugs, could not give her. She died in his arms. Her identification card, the only physical possession of hers that Haing had, was stolen, and he recovered the photograph on it only by begging one of the officials.

With experiences like these, Haing, like Dith, was a changed, driven man when he finally, in 1980, reached the United States. The two men were closer than they could have imagined, and the performance, if that's the word, that won Haing his Academy

Award, was more of a re-living. When they finally met at the premiere of *The Killing Fields* in New York, Haing told Dith: 'You are me, and I am you.' The director, Roland Joffe, said in an interview that, having met and chosen Haing for the role, he deliberately cast Sam Waterston, a good but not so well-known an actor, as the 'lead', rather than a star like Al Pacino to 'allow the limelight to shift . . . to a non-professional Cambodian actor'.

It's hard to overestimate the effect that the film had in creating and maintaining awareness worldwide of these events in Cambodia, and the phrase 'killing fields' entered the vocabulary. Dith Pran and Haing Ngor did what they could to maintain the momentum, and, as talks began about the withdrawal of the Vietnamese in 1989, ten years after they had driven the Khmer Rouge from power, Dith and Haing decided that this was the time to return, before the fighting started again. The vehicle for the visit was the Cambodian Documentation Commission, led by David Hawk, which the government of Hun Sen had invited. At this point, there had still been no elections in which there had been a choice of candidates.

The Vietnamese, who effectively occupied the country, had installed a regime composed of Democratic Kampuchea officials who had defected from the eastern zone in 1978, and this was predictably accused by its opponents of being a puppet government. Along and across the Thai border, meanwhile, the three resistance factions – one royalist, one founded by a former Prime Minister, Son Sann, and the other the Khmer Rouge – had formed an uneasy and unequal alliance, dominated by Pol Pot and supported by the Chinese, the United States and Thailand.

This had created the bizarre situation in which, despite all that had happened and all that was known of the atrocities during the period from 1975 to 1979, the flag of Democratic Kampuchea still flew at the United Nations in New York, and Khieu Samphan, no less, urbanely argued the case of the Khmer Rouge. Never mind that the Vietnamese had saved the country from further horror by invading; this was an illegal act, not to be tolerated by the international community. America's enemy could not be seen as a white knight.

So, a number of interests coincided in this trip. Dith and Haing wanted to publicize Khmer Rouge atrocities as a matter of urgency, because once the Vietnamese withdrew, the poorly equipped Cambodian army would have to face the Khmer Rouge alone, and the latter were already promising a fresh offensive. Hun Sen wanted the moral legitimacy in preparation for the huge United Nations operation that was looming. This would pave the way in two or three years for the elections, which Hun Sen of course was determined to win. And then there were the media. In the United States, ABC Television were launching a high-profile news feature series called *Prime Time*, hosted by their current star, Diane Sawyer. They had decided that the return of Dith and Haing would be a strong subject for one of the hour-long programmes and were, in fact, paying for most of the visit. At the same time, David Puttnam was taking his film to Phnom Penh for its Cambodian premiere. Dith was now working for the *New York Times* and was writing this up for the paper's magazine. Roger and I, as suggested by Haing, were doing the story for the *Sunday Times Magazine* in London.

After a week in Angkor, Roger and I flew down to Phnom Penh to meet the plane, which like most aircraft in those days was arriving from Saigon. The chartered Air Vietnam flight was late, the airport almost deserted. We sat and talked with Sydney Schanberg, who was waiting for Dith. Now working for the New York newspaper *Newsday*, he was covering the premiere of the film. The flight landed, and we drove into the city, to the Monorom, one of the few hotels that were open and functioning.

Communications worked poorly, both with the outside world and internally. But by word of mouth the news gradually spread that both Dith Pran and Haing Ngor were in town. As we walked around, or just sat in the lobby of the Monorom, people would appear, old friends, relations, individually and in small groups, and the reunions were usually emotional. With Dith it was different. He was much more reserved, but then also he had a job to do for his newspaper.

'You see what he's doing, don't you?' remarked Roger. 'Every time the situation looks like it's getting uncomfortable, he holds up either his notebook or his camera. It's as if he's protecting himself from the emotion.'

Although Haing had played the part of Dith Pran, and had had his own horrible experiences, their personalities were by no means similar, and here in Phnom Penh this was causing an uncomfortable problem. Haing's emotions were there for all to see. He was excitable by nature, cried when he met his brother for the first time in fifteen years on the tarmac at Pochentong airport, spoke and gestured dramatically – in short, he was good for the camera. This, crudely put, was the issue. Yes, Hun Sen had invited them both, along with the other members of the Cambodian Documentation Commission, but the publicity engine that really counted here was ABC Television, for which this was to be a big budget special. They were footing a large part of the bill, and strong television was wanted. Dith Pran's own story for the *New York Times*, and the one that Roger and I were doing, were very much supporting features to the main production.

And all was not going perfectly well. Neal Shapiro, the producer, explained the dilemma. There would be the usual interviews, backgrounders of city life around Phnom Penh, Dith's visit to his family home in Siem Reap, and the predictable reminders of the atrocities – namely a tour of Tuol Sleng and the memorial at Chung Ek, the principal killing fields near the city. But this being television they needed, as he reasonably put it, strong and visible emotions on camera. They were not getting these from Dith, and it was hard to broach such a horrible subject with him. No one could say, 'Look, Dith, can't you cry for us like Haing?' But, without being callous, Neal hoped he would all the same. The next day we were scheduled to drive out to Chung Ek, where there were hundreds of human skulls on display – execution victims – and Neal anticipated that this would be the occasion, if any, on which Dith would react. Chung Ek, however, had been developed and tidied up, and was no longer the stark scene of horror that had been filmed and photographed shortly after the Vietnamese invasion. Another friend of mine, Roland Neveu, based in Bangkok, had photographed the skulls, some of them still wearing blindfolds, when they had first been exhumed, and it was this kind of shocking image that Neal had in mind. Now, however, the skulls had been collected and stacked neatly behind glass. This was horrible in its own way, but the sanitization would work against the television filming.

As it turned out, there was an alternative. Back in Siem Reap, Roger recalled that in 1982 he had been shown the killing fields that were in sight of the towers of Angkor Wat, and with Khon's help we went to find them again. The front line after the North Vietnamese Army had taken the temples was between Angkor Wat and the town, with trenches. In April 1975, when the Khmer Rouge entered Siem Reap, the killings began, and many of the victims were buried here, a little north and west of the Welcome sign. What I didn't know at the time was that Dith had seen this in 1979 on his escape from the Khmer Rouge labour camp. He made his way first to his home town, Siem Reap, to find his family before continuing his trek to the Thai border. Only his mother and his younger sister had survived. Dith's father had died of starvation, three brothers had been executed, as had his elder sister with her husband and two children. He asked where the bodies were buried, and was taken to these killing fields nearby. As elsewhere, like Chung Ek, the Vietnamese forced Khmer Rouge cadre to exhume the bones from the trenches as punishment.

Ten years later, little had changed. About 100 metres down a dusty track just after the Welcome sign was a yellowish two-storey building, pock-marked with bullet holes like most of the other abandoned structures on the outskirts of town. It had been built in the 1950s as a hospital and warehouse for the Chinese who came to build the airport. Most of the ground floor was open on two sides. One end was almost filled with a large, low wooden platform, and on this were piled hundreds of skulls and other bones, interspersed with scraps and strips of old cloth. Local cattle had been using the room as a shelter, and the bare concrete floor was spattered with their dung. As we entered, we startled a thin, undernourished cow, and she skidded clumsily to escape, kicking one of the several skulls that lay on the ground. It made a hollow clack as it bounced, the sort of sound you'd expect

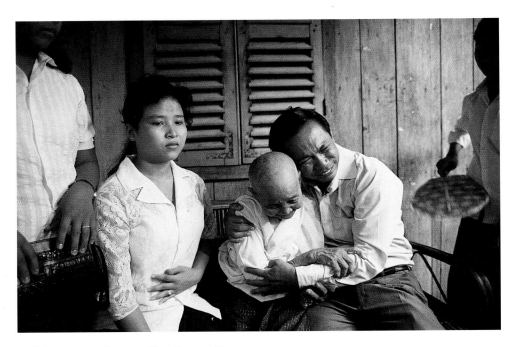

Dith Pran returns home to Siem Reap, 1989

from a dried-out coconut. We picked up the skulls scattered around the floor and replaced them on the platform with the others.

When Neal announced the shoot at Chung Ek, which he had not yet seen, we took him on one side. It was a macabre question of which location was the more horrible. We were all scheduled in two days time to fly up to Siem Reap for filming at Angkor, where Dith had been a guide, at his house and at a nearby monastery where there was to be a memorial ceremony for the lost members of his family.

'If Chung Ek doesn't give you what you need, Neal', I said, 'there's this other place', and described the Angkor killing field to him.

'No, unfortunately it doesn't work like that', he explained. 'In a situation like this, you only get one opportunity. If you think the Angkor site is the one, we'll do only that.'

This put me on the spot, but it seemed the right thing to do. We agreed to mention this to no one else for the time being, least of all to the Foreign Ministry, whose minders might object to such a raw, unpleasant setting. In principle we were all on the same side, but they might, we guessed, have felt that the neglect of the Angkor killing fields reflected poorly on the government. There was nothing to be gained, in any case, from giving advance notice – someone might even tidy it up, as would inevitably happen later.

On the day, the whole group drove in one small bus from Siem Reap airport into town and then up the long, straight road to the temples. As we reached the Welcome sign, I asked the driver to turn into the track and stop. Neal then explained the situation and asked Dith and Haing if they would agree to being filmed there. They did. We parked a little way from the old Chinese hospital and walked. The two men stood and looked, then Haing sat down and spoke to camera. Dith joined him on the edge of the low platform, next to the skulls, and burst into tears. As he later wrote:

A map of Cambodia assembled from the skulls and bones of victims of Tuol Sleng

For the first time since my arrival, what I see before me is too painful, and I break down completely. These are my relatives, friends and neighbours, I keep thinking. I know my father had died slowly of starvation at home, but I don't know how or where my brothers and sister and some of their families were killed. All I know is they were probably killed nearby. It is a long time before I am calm again. And then I am able, with my bare hands, to rearrange the skulls and bones so that they are not scattered about.

No one else speaks, the television camera silently records. After a while, everyone except Dith and Haing leaves, and we stand about in the field awkwardly.

Afterwards, we go to Dith's old home, on the other side of the narrow river from the Conservancy. His parents' house is typical of the region, built of wood and raised high off the ground on stilts. A steep wooden staircase leads up to a half-open verandah. Dith climbs this with his sister, and meets his mother's only surviving sister. He cries again at this emotional reunion, as I sit across the narrow table from them. This, and I can sense it at the time, is the cover shot for the magazine. Later, as the male head of the family, Dith leads a memorial ceremony at the local monastery, with four monks officiating. Haing also attends, as does most of the village. There is some sense of catharsis; what needed to be done was done, and for the American television as well.

The only sour note occurs at the end of this, at lunch in the Grand Hotel in town. David Hawk had asked me, if I had time, to shoot some black-and-white that the Commission could use, and I had done this at the Chinese hospital (I normally shoot colour). I handed him the roll of film across the table. Sitting next to him was an American photographer called McCurry, who had been covering the same story for the *New York Times*. He looked up and asked 'What's that?' I explained.

'You can't do that!', McCurry said in a tense, high-pitched voice. Puzzled (though I'm used to freelance photographer paranoia), I asked: 'Why on earth not?'

'Because this is an assignment', he said, 'I don't want pictures going anywhere else.' Roger and I looked at each other. I was ready to make a scathing remark when David shrugged, said 'Never mind', and handed me back the film. Paranoia certainly did seem to be part of this mean-spiritedness when, the next day, while we were waiting in the Council of Ministers in Phnom Penh for an interview with Hun Sen, the photographer presented me with a scrap of paper on which had been written in a childlike hand a statement that I would delay publishing any pictures until his had appeared. 'Michael', he said, 'I'd like you to sign this.'

'Don't be ridiculous', I replied. Roger was furious and dismissive at the same time.

A VISIT TO S-21

Later that day we visited Tuol Sleng, the local name for the detention and torture centre known officially as s-21. Originally a high school for the surrounding suburb of Tuol Sleng, the building, with frangipani trees in the grounds, was converted into an interrogation centre as early as 1975. This was part of a programme of hunting enemies within the Party. In all, nearly 20,000 prisoners passed through s-21, where they were made to write their biographies, then tortured to extract the 'truth'. Only 200 prisoners were brought here in the first year, but 2,250 in 1976, then 5,000 in 1977, and more in 1978. Almost all were executed after interrogation, and to the factory workers who remained locally, the barbed-wire-festooned school was known as the 'place of entering, not leaving'. Only seven people survived.

The horror was discovered only when it was reached by the invading Vietnamese troops. Conflict between Democratic Kampuchea and Vietnam had been brewing right from the start, with a number of Cambodian territorial claims. There was, in any case, the underlying resentment, historical and ethnic, of Vietnam. Border skirmishes and raids, many brutal, notched up the tension. In 1977, following the death of Mao Zedong, Chinese foreign policy shifted to an anti-Soviet stance, and Vietnam was

Prisoners at Tuol Sleng photographed on their induction

Torture room at Tuol Sleng

seen as pro-Soviet. Cambodia was drawn into this and encouraged to play its role as a Chinese ally, with a huge increase in military supplies authorized by Beijing.

The Vietnamese response to this new alliance was a military offensive at the end of 1977, briefly occupying a zone 30 kilometres deep, withdrawing with thousands of hostages. Pol Pot's reaction was not only to break off diplomatic relations, but to begin purges among party officials and military officers in the eastern zone. To escape these, which swelled the numbers at Tuol Sleng, many fled to Vietnam. The sequence of provocation and counter-provocation continued until, finally, on Christmas Day 1978, the Vietnamese army invaded in force, meeting little resistance. Their original plan had been to secure the eastern part of the country, but at the end of December they decided instead to capture Phnom Penh. The speed with which they achieved this – by 7 January – took the regime by surprise, and evacuation of the city was as urgent and chaotic as it had been by Lon Nol four years earlier, Pol Pot leaving at the last minute by helicopter.

For Tuol Sleng this had an important repercussion – the guards had no time to destroy the voluminous paperwork, detailing admissions and confessions. It was this archive, collated and translated by investigators such as Tim Carney and Steve Heder, that became the hard evidence for the crimes committed by the regime. Among these archives were photographs – of prisoners holding numbers as they arrived, and also of bodies after interrogation. The Vietnamese and the new government were determined to make this a display of Khmer Rouge atrocities, and it became the Museum of the Genocidal Crimes of Pol Pot.

This was my second visit. It was truly one of the most disturbing of experiences, and if ever there was a place that retained the imprint of past events and could replay them for the visitor, it was Tuol Sleng, a Southeast Asian Auschwitz that specialized in pain. On this occasion, in fact, neither Roger nor I wanted to repeat the experience, and we waited by the gate. We had with us as an interpreter Samnang Siv – it was at her wedding in Massachusetts that I had first met Haing. Like every

Cambodian, she had a story. Hers was that her father, a senior military officer under the Lon Nol government, had responded to the call by the Khmer Rouge for all officials and professionals to come and help rebuild the shattered country. This was typical Khmer Rouge duplicity. He reported and was never heard from again. Samnang was clearly torn between entering the school and not.

'You don't have to do that', advised Roger, knowing the effect of the place.

'I think I ought to', she said. The discussion continued for a few minutes. She finally went in after the others, and there discovered what had happened to her father. His was one of the hundreds of photographs lining the walls. She emerged distraught. Roger tried his best to comfort her. I could think of nothing at all to say. One of the young Cambodian women working for the Ministry talked to her, saying that she had once seen her brother's decapitated head on a table. Everyone indeed had a story, and at times each seemed to be worse than the one before.

In 1996 Haing was driving home late one evening, in Los Angeles. As he reached the open carport, he was confronted by three young professional thieves. It was a Sunday night and the three members of the Oriental Lazy Boyz street gang were looking for someone to rob. At gunpoint they took his gold Rolex and demanded his locket – which contained the photograph of Huoy, the one ripped from her identification card that he had had to beg for at the Khmer Rouge camp almost 20 years earlier. Haing refused, and was shot. The casual violence of youth, so easily learned in both revolutionary Cambodia and in American cities, ended Haing's life as it had so many of his countrymen.

THE VIETNAMESE WITHDRAWAL

The only solution acceptable to the international community was a verified withdrawal of the Vietnamese troops and elections monitored by the United Nations. The flight on which Roger and I first arrived in Cambodia was at the very start of this process.

Heroic sculptures of Vietnamese Army liberators, Phnom Penh, 1989

Government troops passing through Angkor on their way to the front, 1991

On the last night of our first visit to Angkor, the hotel suddenly filled up with military – Vietnamese and Cambodian officers. This was the Grand, now tarted up by the new owners, Raffles, then faded and decrepit. Until that evening we, and two reclusive Russian engineers, had been the only residents, the staff taking it in turns to sleep in the lobby with their м-16s. We had seen little of the Cambodian army apart from the occasional tank trundling past the temples towards the north (the daily artillery barrage from positions several kilometres beyond Preah Khan indicated regular engagements), and nothing at all of the Vietnamese. They were keeping a very low profile in these last days, although frustratingly for us they still had a position on Bakheng hill, which kept me from getting a shot I wanted.

This evening, however, was their final leaving party. The withdrawal had begun. Although we were unexpected company, the Vietnamese officers were gracious enough to invite us to join the party, which consisted of a local group performing Santana passably, a group of girls from a nearby village for some fairly innocent dancing, and huge quantities of beer and cognac. The last almost did for me, as there was no way to refuse the toasts, to which there was no limit. Fortunately, one of the waiters came to my rescue. I had a mouthful of cognac which at this stage in the drinking would have been foolish to swallow. He moved over to one of the rear windows of the dining room and caught my attention. I picked my way carefully over to where he was standing. The long windows were an old-fashioned design, opening by pivoting horizontally. He swung one open, giving me a clear shot to the flowerbed below. We repeated this little performance for the rest of the evening.

The Khmer Rouge had celebrated the occasion the previous night by firing a Chinese rocket that had exploded a little short of the hotel, a day too early for the Vietnamese, but enough to jolt me awake. This was exactly what most Cambodians feared – that the vacuum between the Vietnamese military presence and the arrival of the UN troops, still a couple of years away, would attract a new Khmer Rouge offensive that the poorly equipped government forces would be unable to cope with. This is why Haing and

Dith made their trip. In the event, the Americans withdrew their support for the non-Communist opposition factions, which encouraged the Chinese to reduce *their* support for the Khmer Rouge, who failed to make any serious inroads.

UNTAC

Following the Paris power-sharing agreements of 1991, the UN operation lumbered slowly and expensively into Cambodia as UNTAC – the United Nations Transitional Authority in Cambodia. By the time that the mission withdrew in October 1993, it had become the most costly exercise in UN history, at two billion US dollars. Much of this went on engorged salaries and expenses that left ordinary Cambodians bewildered but, with their long experience of more traditional Asian forms of corruption and pocket-lining, not altogether surprised. Military and police units from all over the world descended on the country, few of them with any knowledge of Cambodia, some clearly in it for the money. The acronyms chosen for the various national battalions used the suffix 'bat', and Bulgbat, the Bulgarian contingent, was conspicuous for its involvement in vice. The Khmer Rouge refused to be monitored, took more territory in the northwest, and began massacres of Vietnamese civilians. Government security forces also took the opportunity to undertake political assassinations, and the UNTAC forces were powerless to prevent this.

This countryside policing, however, at least made it safer to travel over much of the country than it had been for many years. I took the opportunity to spend a night near the small temple of Banteay Srei, Malraux's favourite, in the company of Bangbat – the Bangladeshi army. Banteay Srei had long been in a disputed area, and the Khmer Rouge were still in control a little to the north, beyond the Kulen hills, but here at least the villages were enjoying a taste of protected normality. My host was a Captain Shafiqur Reza, from Dacca, and on our arrival he sent a section of infantry to escort Khon and me to the temple for sunset. The soldiers patrolled the moat with their old British .303 rifles as we

Government troops returning from an engagement, Siem Reap, 1991

took our photographs. Seeing them with their ancient weapons and in what was essentially British army Second World War battledress made me think of weekend exercises with the school cadet corps. It too had been equipped mainly from war surplus, but that had been 30 years earlier. The large tent that I shared with Captain Reza was an unmistakable antique – it was date-stamped 1946.

But despite their outdated supplies, and not having been paid for weeks, the Bangladeshis were the model of efficiency and courtesy. After dark, Captain Reza invited me to join him in a little kiosk that he had had built in camp. A sergeant appeared with a tray of hot, freshly made samosas. This being a Muslim unit, I knew not to expect the only thing that could have perfected the evening, a cold beer, but then the sergeant returned with a chilled can of Heineken. Reza took his leave for a few minutes to make an inspection, and I rocked back in my chair in this unexpected luxury. There was a sudden blinding flash of light, followed immediately by an appallingly loud explosion. I immediately dived to the ground. There was a moment of silence, no debris falling, nothing nearby damaged. I picked myself up and followed the soldiers running towards the entrance of the camp. There, just outside, visible in the several torchlights, was a huge artillery piece with its Cambodian army crew. Reza was there. 'Very naughty', he said, 'They've put themselves right next to our camp for protection. They know they're not even supposed to be firing. But what can we do?'

It was a Soviet 130 mm field gun, provided by the Vietnamese, and the Cambodians were using it to shell Khmer Rouge positions on the other side of the Kulen hills, some 30 kilometres distant. Fingers in our ears, we watched the Cambodians load another round and prepare to fire. The muzzle flash from the long barrel lit up the surrounding trees, and the blast was followed by a piercing screech, diminishing in volume and pitch as the shell sped off in its high parabola across the hills.

Yet despite this kind of incident, and much worse, the national elections did take place when they were intended, in July 1993, and at least 90 per cent of the registered voters voted. Not, of

Hun Sen at a press conference, 1989

Sihanouk returns to Phnom Penh, 1992, beneath an idealized portrait

course, that there were any neat endings. It was a royalist opposition party that gained the most votes, yet Hun Sen's ruling party refused to accept the results, and created what was effectively a sham coalition. A violent coup in 1996 further weakened the opposition. Nevertheless, the elections of 1998 were free and fair, as were those of 2001. Hun Sen's strong and skilful control of government may leave much to be desired, but has at least brought a measure of stability. Sihanouk was made king again, but without the power that he had enjoyed before, and he spends less and less time in the country.

The Khmer Rouge hung on with remarkable tenacity, continuing to purge themselves by means of assassinations, and to kidnap and murder the occasional foreigner with no regard for the political consequences, dwindling in power and size. In their final stronghold, Anlong Veng in the forested foothills of the Dangreks, they finally turned against their ageing leader, Pol Pot. After a show trial in a jungle hut, he was condemned to life imprisonment in his small house nearby, and died shortly afterwards, in 1998. With the new road just completed, visitors to nearby Preah Vihear can now stop and enjoy the sights and eat at the recently opened restaurant. From Ancient Angkor via Tuol Sleng to Pol Pot's deathbed, the tourist circuit now quite neatly encloses Cambodia's history. And if you want fully to absorb the last nostalgic days of the Khmer Rouge, there is a guest-house where you can spend the night. Although not actually in Pol Pot's bungalow. Or at least, not yet.

v From the Peanut Gallery: Cambodia, the Movie and Classical Dance

The year 2001 was a minor landmark in the motion picture industry, the year in which there appeared a major Hollywood film based not on a novel, a play, a real-life event or any of the usual plot catalysts, but on a mindless computer game. Childish certainly, but *Tomb Raider* had been an enormous success. As a Bangkok-based film reviewer reported it, 'For several years, nerds, geeks, yuppies, students and others have drooled whenever computer heroine Lara Croft shot and kick-boxed her way through updated tomb raider videogames.' Now, with a star to match – Angelina Jolie, whose opinion of the game character was 'She's everything I think I'd like to be . . . really bold and funny and loyal, and she's got that wit' – what better real-life location than Angkor? As the reviewer breathlessly continued, 'Robobabe Lara Croft, with her mouse-enhanced bod, has leaped through cyberspace into the twisted jungle temple ruins of 12th century Angkor Wat . . .'.

The movies have come to Cambodia, and it's all location, location, location. Until the world is thoroughly familiar with the sights of Angkor (this may not take too long at the current rate of progress), jungles and ruins continue to make great movie sets. In the winter of 2002–3, The French director Jean-Jacques Annaud, who made *Seven Years in Tibet* and *Enemy at the Gates*, used a range of locations from Phnom Penh to Mondulkiri to the previously untouched temple of Beng Mealea for his new film, *Two Brothers*. The siblings in question are tiger cubs who are separated, lead very different lives and are finally united. For this, 30 trained tigers of different ages were imported with their handlers from around the world – the most that Cambodia's depleted forests had seen in many years.

Major feature films mean cash and a flurry of local employ-

164

ment, a potential boost to tourism because of the publicity, and disruption. The Phnom Penh post reported:

> As Angelina Jolie jumped and dived around Angkor over the course of eight days of shooting her role as *Tomb Raider* femme fatale Lara Croft, the film's depiction of brightly dressed monks and seemingly idyllic villages populated by people inexplicably wearing traditional Vietnamese hats – much to the annoyance of the locally hired extras – showed little awareness or sensitivity to the reality of modern Cambodia.

Princess Rattana-Devi, Sihanouk's granddaughter who, like the old king, has a passion for movies, gave her thoughts on what *Tomb Raider* might do for the tourist industry. 'Films help sell Cambodia and we need tourism for the economy, so that is good', she said,

> I am happy and sad about it. I know how Cambodians are suffering because they are poor. I am not against tourism because it is so important for my country. Yet I cannot help but be nostalgic for the days when you could go to the temples in Siem Reap and be alone. The little children selling Coke at the temple are cute, but I am not so sure that they are growing up to respect a sacred place.

Cute is not quite the description I would use for the hordes of village kids who now swarm around the tour buses hawking anything that their parents can lay their hands on, from postcards to carvings to pirated guidebooks (mine included). But the princess was echoing that old royalist sentiment that her grandfather indulged in – Angkor as royal playground. Indeed, Angkor as a royal film set. The temples in particular, and Cambodia in general, have had an interesting and at times bizarre involvement with the movies. In 2001 *Tomb Raider* was just the latest in a line of feature films that sometimes exploited the country's scenery and history – and sometimes interfered with its politics.

In 1965 President Johnson decided, finally, to take a stand on Vietnam. 'I have asked the commanding general, General Westmoreland, what more he needs to meet this mounting aggression', he announced on US television, choosing midday for the smallest possible audience. 'He has told me. And we will meet his needs.' The troops and the equipment and weapons began to pour into Vietnam on an unprecedented scale, and the pressure was mounting on Cambodia. Sihanouk's efforts since the beginning of the 1960s had been directed at keeping the country out of the war. 'We are like a country caught between the hammer and the anvil', he said in an interview, 'a country that would very much like to remain the last haven of peace in Southeast Asia.'

In this crisis year, Sihanouk's plan of action was . . . to make movies. Between 1965 and 1969 he succeeded in completing nine feature films, which would have been an achievement even for a professional director, let alone a head of state facing a cataclysm. This was displacement activity on a massive, megalomaniac scale, bizarre even for a ruler known for his fads (which had included horse-riding and magazine publishing). Sihanouk's movie-making was stopped by his overthrow in 1970, but it undoubtedly played a part in his downfall by distracting him so much.

The reasons for Sihanouk's sudden enthusiasm for the cinema were just as irrational: jealousy and pique. These were both inspired by, of all things, the British film of Joseph Conrad's novel *Lord Jim*, starring Peter O'Toole, which had just opened. The producer and director, Richard Brooks, had decided to set a crucial part of the film in Angkor, and had secured permission to shoot there in 1964. All well and good, but the critical and commercial success of *Lord Jim* rankled with Sihanouk. The preamble to the premiere of his rather hurriedly shot first feature, *Apsara*, gave vent to his feelings:

For a film producer (even one of real talent) what is Cambodia? The ruins of Angkor . . . and that is all. So, a run-of-the-mill script is hurriedly written, one or two flashy stars are hired, one adds a mixture of eroticism and violence, advance promotion dwells on the same old hackneyed themes (. . . scorpions lurking in boots . . . the poverty of the people . . . etc.) and the whole lot is put in motion. That is the image of Cambodia current in the four corners of the globe.

And that was the image that Sihanouk wanted to correct. More than this, he was furious at the off-the-cuff remarks made by the star, Peter O'Toole, who hated everything about the experience and the country. Location filming had begun in Hong Kong, which O'Toole also loathed; he described it as 'Manchester with slanted eyes'. This set the tone for when the company moved to Cambodia. There was already at Angkor a small hotel opposite the monument, an annexe to the Grand Hotel called the Hôtel des Ruines (later totally demolished by the Khmer Rouge). Brooks reportedly spent $600,000 adding a 47-room wing to accommodate the cast and crew, and the dyspeptic O'Toole naturally had something to say about this.

'That hotel!' he fumed to *Life* magazine. 'More expensive than Claridge's! Ten flaming quid a night and a poxy room at that. Nicest thing you could say about the food was that it was grotesque.'

And then Sihanouk himself turned up. 'He started yelling the usual anti-British crud', said O'Toole. 'I walked up to him and said, "I couldn't agree with you more. I'm Irish meself."'

Brooks had allowed for twelve weeks of shooting, but halfway through he was approached by a mysterious Frenchman, who advised him to finish and leave by 12 of March. For some reason Brooks took this seriously, as did O'Toole, and the work schedule was doubled. The company left Cambodia on 3 March, and a week later mobs in Phnom Penh attacked the British and US embassies. Sihanouk went on to the radio to denounce the film company, of all people, as 'Western imperialist invaders'. O'Toole was included in this as being a part of the conspiracy by the West to undermine Cambodia. I wonder if O'Toole was amused or horrified to learn that he set in motion a train of events that led to the prince fiddling with his movie cameras while the country descended into chaos and ruin. Or even knew.

Sihanouk took his art very seriously, but the films were banal fantasies. Milton Osborne, his unauthorized biographer, attended the first showing of the first film *Apsara*, in its unedited form. The audience was first reminded of the need for this portrayal of Cambodia, namely the unforgivable falsehoods of *Lord Jim*: 'Is it any longer possible to ignore such ineptitudes, such errors, whether voluntary or otherwise? Certainly not, and the Chief of State, more than any other, has felt this deeply. And so, once again, faithful to his reputation as the "Pioneer Prince", he has taken up the challenge'. Described as *une féerie*, the story-line of this 'real picture of present-day Cambodia' involved an old roué abandoning his mistress to pursue a dancer with the royal ballet. The dancer, however, was in love with an Air Force pilot, and, although a marriage takes place, it is not consummated. The pilot is wounded while defending his nation from the Vietnamese and Americans and is reunited with his love. The old man marries his mistress.

The most real thing about this film is its cast, which includes Sihanouk's daughter, son and two generals, one the Minister for Foreign Affairs and Planning, the other the Commander of the Cambodian Air Force. It also starred for the climactic action scene most of the Air Force's helicopters, leaving wounded Cambodian troops stranded on the northern border. Vehicles included a Facel Vega, Jaguar, Cadillac convertible and a Mercedes – this in a country principally of cycle rickshaws, all of which had been banished from the streets during shooting. Quite what the villagers in the Khmer countryside made of all these goings on (Sihanouk commanded that the film be shown nationwide) is hard to imagine, but it and its successors must have been useful fertilizer for the revolutionary arguments of the growing insurgency.

Spurred on by the experience, although blind to the reaction, Sihanouk went on to write, produce and direct more dire entertainments, including *The Little Prince*, *Joie de vivre*, and the all too aptly titled late film, *Crépuscule* (*Twilight*). In some of these he also took an acting role, playing variously a general, a wounded soldier, an intelligence agent, a Japanese colonel and a forest sprite. And, a sign of how his art was improving, Sihanouk's final two films won the grand prize, a solid gold statue, at the Phnom Penh International Film Festival. At the last of these, his entry was the only competitor. The results were embarrassing to most thoughtful Cambodians, although the sycophantic British diplomat Malcolm MacDonald, whose fondest memory was of water-skiing with the prince on the West Baray at Angkor, compared *Joie de vivre* with the Sistine Chapel.

WAR MOVIES

The first feature-film appearance of Cambodia at war is in Coppola's *Apocalypse Now*. The plot is a miniature odyssey in which the hero, a cynical US army assassin, travels up a river from its mouth near the Mekong delta in search of his target, a much-decorated war hero who has gone renegade in the depths of the Cambodian jungle. Coppola based the film on a story by Joseph Conrad – his most famous work, *Heart of Darkness*. This made it the second time that Conrad was brought to Cambodia, *Lord Jim* being the first. It was coincidental, because Conrad had in mind very different locations for his two works, and indeed never featured Cambodia in any of his extensive writings on Southeast Asia. Or rather, in both cases the directors had seen the potential in the atmosphere of decay, ruin and violence.

Coppola's choice was particularly apt. Conrad set his tale, published in 1899, in the Congo of the late nineteenth century. This was then the ironically named Congo Free State, a dark and terrible place in which King Leopold II of Belgium personally exploited the riches in rubber. This operation was conducted with a savage thoroughness in which millions of Congolese died, possibly up to two-thirds of the population. When the rubber quotas were not met, right hands were chopped off. The atrocities were largely unreported until Roger Casement's investigation, upon which the other European countries forced Leopold to give up his private horror show.

Conrad made this his heart of darkness in three senses: a journey into the unknown forests of the 'dark continent', another into a region of cruelty and inhumanity, and finally into the depths of one man's dark soul – Kurtz, the man at the end of the river, who has seen the worst of which man is capable and has seen the worst in himself. The story ends with his dying words, 'The horror! The horror!' All of which translated effectively to Cambodia in *its* darkest days. The veteran set designer George Nelson based Kurtz's headquarters on the face-tower temples built by Jayavarman VII (this was built, and the film shot, in the Philippines), and the *montagnard* irregulars behave with suitable barbarism, decorating the buildings with the decapitated heads of their enemy. Marlon Brando, as Kurtz, gives an odd, barely coherent performance, mainly in shadow. Overweight, his head smoothly shaved, the thick-necked Brando curiously resembles the fleshy, burly king Jayavarman VII, well-known from several statues, and probably the inspiration for those face-towers.

But the film that really put Cambodia on the international map was *The Killing Fields*, as already described. The reaction of Sihanouk, so touchy on matters of national pride, is not on record, but that of Princess Rattana-Devi has that depressing ring of those who would really much rather put all that unpleasantness behind them: ' . . . I am concerned about the country's image in these movies. Because of films like *The Killing Fields*, Cambodia is like a beautiful woman who is badly dressed. If it were up to me, I would be very selective about what movies can shoot [*sic*] in the country.' It's not clear whether the Princess realized that the film was in fact shot in Thailand, or that films that tend to show nations 'not in a flattering light', as she put it, are usually made elsewhere for obvious reasons.

But then what was there to flatter? *The Killing Fields* certainly engaged Phnom Penh audiences when it was first shown there. The day after we returned from our sad but effective filming in Siem Reap with Haing and Dith, I went to a screening in the country's one cinema on Monivong Boulevard. The premiere had been the previous week, when David Puttnam had brought over a print, but today the special event was that Haing and Dith

The premiere of *The Killing Fields* in Phnom Penh, 1989

would be on stage to introduce it. The cinema was packed, as far as I could see with quite ordinary Cambodians, not the political elite. After Haing's impassioned speech, the film began.

I went first to the projection booth, which was also where the dubbing would take place, in real time. Next to the projectionist sat a man and a woman, with a microphone on the desk between them. Each had a large sheaf of papers, all handwritten in Khmer, and I realized that this was the newly translated script. The dubbing was as simple and disruptive as it could be. The full English soundtrack was run, music and sound effects included, until a point of dialogue was reached. Then, either the man or the woman, depending on the gender of the character speaking, flipped a switch close to the microphone, cutting off the sound completely while they read their lines. They played all the parts, without attempting the nuance of varied accents. None of this, however, distracted the audience, who were riveted. I went down the steps to the theatre and joined them. All the seats were taken, and I sat in the aisle. By the time I sat down, the film had reached the battle scene, full of gunfire, explosions and chaos. I was interested to see how the audience, most of whom had lived through similar incidents, were taking this. To a Western audience this was the high-adrenaline scene of battlefield adventure, but the Cambodians, who knew about this personally, must have a different perspective. I looked around. All the faces were transfixed, but at the same time expressionless. No one flinched or fidgeted.

Now, this is the scene in which, as I remembered, we get our first glimpse of the Khmer Rouge, so I knew what was coming. There is a shot from the front line across the rice-fields, the smoke from fires and explosions drifting across the screen. Then the smoke clears, and in the distance are the small, black-clad figures of the Khmer Rouge troops advancing. There was suddenly one of the strangest sounds I have ever heard, a huge, collective intake of breath. I turned around. The entire audience, in unison, made a great indrawn sigh. Nothing else, no individual noises. There was both a restraint and an intensity that impressed me; not something I would care to hear again. I knew the remainder of the film in any case – I left.

172

It was inevitable that eventually the country would attract film-makers, usually less for an interest in Cambodia, its culture and its problems than for the visual spectacle. This was, after all, what had drawn Richard Brooks here for the pivotal setting of *Lord Jim*. The monuments, the archetypal Southeast Asian landscape of the Western imagination, the old-fashionedness, are all very easy on the camera. I had an opportunity to see something of the Hollywood approach in the first feature-length film to be shot (partly) in post-war Cambodia. Called *Baraka* (an ancient Sufi word meaning blessing, or the breath or essence of life), it was a film without actors, without even dialogue, that attempted through images and music an exploration of, as the producer Mark Magidson put it, 'man's interconnectedness, spirituality, his capacity for destruction, and mortality'.

I was just finishing a publicity tour in the United States for my first book on Angkor when Mark tracked me down. Few other photographs of the temples were in circulation at the time, and the director, Ron Fricke, thought he could see some of the images working as film sequences. There were also the logistical and bureaucratic difficulties of getting a crew, and their 65 cases of equipment, to Cambodia. I happily agreed to help; it was another opportunity to return. This was 70 mm film rather than the usual 35 mm, and the cameras were massive. One had a small brass plaque identifying the last film it had been used on, *Ryan's Daughter* (1970). The other, built almost from scratch in Mark's engineering company, was a computer-controlled machine that would perform long, complicated moves on the 30-foot rail that the crew also brought. One of Ron's specialities was time-lapse photography (he had been director of photography on *Koyaanisquatsi*, which had a not dissimilar theme, and also directed *Chronos*, an IMAX film). The computer-controlled camera and its rails were to be put to use in ten-hour, all-night tracking shots. For this, we timed our visit for the full moon.

Although the Cambodian footage was to be a small part of the whole, Ron wanted everything. Each location that we recce'd was better for him than the last. Under the full moon, the atmosphere

173

of the filming was decidedly strange. There was still a nightly curfew in force, although we had been exempted, and the silence at the Bayon was almost complete. Every minute the camera would advance to a new frame with a click and a whirr, and every so often there was the gentle whoosh of a bat executing manoeuvres between the face-towers. Ron was also drawn to Preah Khan, and in particular its long axis running east to west. The succession of doorways recedes into the distance, and he conceived the idea of a single time-lapse tracking shot in which the camera would appear to float through these openings from the entrance to the stupa in the middle.

This was easier said than done, since it would involve building and dismantling sets of rail as the camera moved slowly over the course of a few hours, without any jarring. The solution was to turn the camera upside down and run it backwards (I always had difficulty in understanding how this produced a forward-moving sequence when it was projected, but that's what it did). This meant gathering all the carpenters we could find in town, and a considerable amount of timber, because the sections of rail had to be supported on one level surface over the succession of stone door sills. Ron became so enthusiastic about this shot that he lost sense of time – or rather, didn't care – and we had to change the flight that we had chartered from Phnom Penh. Air Kampuchea's aircraft were in short supply at the time, and this was short notice. From the airport we made contact with the airline's director in the capital, and he was scathing. 'Foreigners don't keep their word', he shouted, and flatly refused to entertain the idea. We apologized, bargained, offered more money and eventually succeeded in delaying for an extra day.

The filming continued, Ron happy as a sandboy. Then, at the end of the following day, as I was packing ready for the morning flight, the line producer, Alton, returned from the site saying that they now needed yet another day. The reaction the next morning at the airport was frank disbelief. 'No', we were told, 'you ordered the plane, you already changed your minds once, and you're going to have pay for it!' All this was translated for us by our Foreign Ministry man, Heng, who winced as he listened to the high-pitched voice squawking from the short-wave radio. And, we were reminded, there was a war going on. What was worse, there were no more aircraft available. We watched the flight arrive, our supposedly empty Antonov. A few Khmer passengers disembarked – they had somehow hitched a lift – it taxied back on to the runway and took off, completely empty. It was a few more days before we managed to hire another.

CAMBODIAN FILMS

Film-making for Cambodians, however, is not so easy. Not least among the difficulties is that, at the time of writing, there is just one cinema in the entire country, the newly restored Vimean Tep on Monivong Boulevard in Phnom Penh. Even this is an improvement, since from 1995 to 2002 there was none at all. Back in the 1960s, the city (though not the country) had a thriving film industry, with an output of some 50 films a year showing in more than 30 cinemas. The Khmer Rouge naturally put a complete stop to this, and many actors and directors were executed or died in the harsh conditions of the work camps. When the Vietnamese invaded and restored peace, there was an attempt to revive film-making, but it did not last long. Imported Thai soap operas and video players proved too strong a competition.

For the few Cambodian directors still determined to make films locally, the process is a world away from Hollywood. Fay Sam Ang's experience with his film *The Snake King's Child* gives some idea of the determination needed. One of the 1960s classics was *Puos Kong Kang*, *The Snake King*, directed by Tea Lim Kun. The plot was from the legend of a *naga* king who seduces a peasant girl, and was a popular success. In 1999 Ang conceived the idea of following this old classic with a new production. His first difficulty was that the Khmer Rouge had destroyed all the prints of the original, so he had to rely on his memory when writing the script.

Then there were the special effects. The one surviving child of the Snake King (a large python borrowed from a local monastery) is a snake-girl with serpentine coils instead of hair. For the makers

175

A small-town barber shop offers David Beckham cuts

of *Tomb Raider*, *Two Brothers* or any modern production, the solution would be straightforward computer-generated imagery. Ang's was glue. The seventeen-year-old actress playing the snake-girl was persuaded to wear a cap on to which were stuck live snakes. 'When she first saw the snakes, she cried and cried', Ang said. Simply showing the film to an audience was no easier. When it was finished in 2001, the Vimean Tep had not yet reopened. The director hired the French Cultural Centre instead, and also arranged projections in the courtyard of a television station.

CAMBODIAN DANCE-DRAMA

And yet Cambodia has an indigenous entertainment that is rich, complex and, perhaps surprisingly, undergoing a very healthy revival. Classical dance, which friezes and bas-reliefs at Angkor show is a tradition that goes back at least a millennium, has a special place in Khmer cultural life. When the country was freed from Khmer Rouge control in the early months of 1980, one of the first decisions was to rebuild the classical dance troupes in Phnom Penh and in the provincial capitals. The arts, and particularly those that had strong connections with courtly tradition, had been specially targeted by the Khmer Rouge. Many dancers died. Pol Pot himself was more than usually aware of the role and culture of the Royal Ballet. His cousin Meak had joined as a dancer, and later his elder brother Loth Suong entered the palace as a clerk, eventually marrying one of the principal dancers, Chea Samy. She, much later, in 1980 when people were trying to pick up the pieces of their lives in the aftermath of the Pol Pot years, was active in finding surviving dancers and re-creating the ballet. In 1934 or 1935 the nine-year-old Saloth Sar arrived in Phnom Penh to live with Meak and Suong, and must certainly have spent time at the palace watching the dancers at work. And as his brother Suong later said, 'The contemptible Pot was a lovely child.'

The classical dance of the court is one of several dance-dramas that, between them, cover the range of Cambodian society, from the village to the palace. Among the ancient traditions of rural life are the ritual dances that accompany the seasonal rhythms of rain, planting, harvest – all designed to bring prosperity. The Trot dance at the time of the Khmer New Year, in the middle of April when the weather is at its hottest, just before the monsoons, is performed by travelling troupes who move from village to village over a number of days, collecting money for their local monastery. Wearing paint or masks, the players represent forest beings, from animals to demons and hunters, and the continuous performance, largely improvised, revolves around a deer hunt. There are also dances to call for rain, to encourage the breeding of buffaloes, to ensure a bountiful catch of fish, and good crops. Theatrical performances include *sbaek thom*, a kind of shadow theatre using large, intricately cut and punched panels of tanned cowhide (the Khmer name means 'large leather'), projected on to a cloth screen; *lakhon khol*, a masked dance performed only by men; and *lakhon luong* ('king's drama'), the classical dance of the court that is performed mainly by women.

In what has traditionally been a largely illiterate society, dance-drama in Cambodia performs a special function. It brings together a surprising range of the arts, including music, choreography, costume, graphic imagery in the intermittently frozen tableaux, and the Khmer literary archive, and presents them in a form that all can appreciate and enjoy. By far the most important literary work in the Khmer language is the *Reamker*, which is the Cambodian version of the great Indian epic, the *Ramayana* – 'the glory of Rama'. Episodes from this huge work form an essential part of the repertoire in *lakhon luong*, *lakhon khol* and *sbaek thom*, what the dance scholar Toni Samantha Phim calls 'a sort of libretto for dramatic performance'.

THE REAMKER

The *Ramayana*, first composed about 550 BC by the poet Valmiki, became one of India's most enduring cultural, social and even political exports to Southeast Asia. In Indian mythology, the god Vishnu – the Preserver and Protector among the Hindu Trinity that also includes Shiva (the Destroyer) and Brahma (the Creator)

178

– descends to Earth a number of times in order to help mankind at times of moral crisis. On each occasion, he takes a different physical form, known as an *avatar*. In one, he is Prince Rama, who, with his wife Sita, brother Lakshmana and monkey prince Hanuman, undergoes epic adventures in a great struggle against the demon king Ravana. Gods, men and monkeys are all involved, and in the original version the tale ranges across the entire known world of India, from Mount Kailash in the Himalayas to the island of Sri Lanka, where the final battle takes place.

The Khmer version is no simple copy. It takes the basic plot, or rather parts of it, and puts this into a Khmer world. Also into a Theravada Buddhist world, because, while the original was firmly embedded in Hindu mythology, it seems that the Khmer poem was not composed until the sixteenth or seventeenth century. By then, the worship of Shiva, occasionally Vishnu and Mahayana Buddhism, all three of which had at one time or another been the state religion, had been overtaken by the more personal Theravada. This is the form of Buddhism practised today in Southeast Asia, in Sri Lanka, Burma, Thailand and Laos as well as Cambodia – less hierarchical, more concerned with the individual's own route to enlightenment, less esoteric ritual. There's a good case for arguing that Theravada ('Teaching of the Elders') works better at the social level of small rural communities, because each male must enter the monastery at some time in his life, even if only for a few weeks – typically the 'rain retreat' of the monsoon.

Not so surprising, then, that the *Reamker* became extremely popular, even though on the face of it the epic's characters are from a very different religion. Underlying the episodes of adventure, war, romance and farce is a basic conflict of good and evil, and an exposition of codes of conduct. Its heroes are virtuous, calm and elegant, its villains unpredictable, grotesque, in chaos. In a flamboyant fairy-tale, the *Reamker* explores the ancient, traditional Cambodian contrast between what is civilized and within the fold (*sruk*) and what is wild and untamed (*prei*). All this makes it sound not so different from *The Lord of the Rings*, but in Cambodia the fantasy is less of an escape than an explanation. Its survival and performance were also assisted, as elsewhere in the region, by its popularity at court. At another level, the *Reamker* presents a strong argument for preserving the *status quo* and for divine, enlightened rule. It is most certainly not a revolutionary tract.

The adventures of Prince Ream (Rama), Sita and younger brother Leak (Lakshmana) begin with their unfair banishment from the kingdom that Ream should have inherited. In the forest, Sita, whom the demon king Reab (Ravana) covets, is abducted through a ruse, and most of the rest of the epic is taken up with the efforts of the two brothers to rescue her from Reab's city, Langka. Many things happen along the way to the final battle, including their involvement with the internal disputes of the monkey kingdom. Ream's friendship with the monkey prince Hanuman – strong, fearless, full of tricks and an inveterate womanizer – brings humour to the tale and ultimately ensures success over the wicked Reab as the monkey troops fight alongside the brave friends.

The Khmer version is highly episodic, being designed essentially for performance, dancers miming and, in some of the dance genres, a narrator reciting the verse. As written, the text was rather formidable, but performances depended on professional storytellers who memorized the epic, and for the most part this is the way that the *Reamker* was presented, by rote learning. However unlikely it sounds that this extremely long epic, taking many performances to cover, could in fact be memorized, there is one famous documented case. François Bizot, before he was captured by the Khmer Rouge, travelled around the countryside researching folk tales and Buddhist texts. In 1969 he came across one man, Ta (grandfather) Chak, who in 1920 at the age of 23 had memorized the entire Reamker from palm leaf manuscripts. Bizot commented: 'He quickly became known and was called to perform at village festivals and then on the stage in the monastery theatres during the big people's celebrations lasting several days.' This was a prodigious feat indeed. The entire recitation took 50 hours, in performances spread over ten days.

The basic cast of the *Reamker* is divided into princes, princesses, ogres and monkeys, and these have become the four character types in classical court dance. The first three of these are played by women, with individual dancers tending to specialize. Typecasting begins at an early age when the young girls begin their training (and the younger the better, the teachers say). Girls with a slim build and round faces train for the princess roles, those with a larger bone structure and longer faces take the parts of princes, while those with a heavier, stronger carriage become ogres. It was only in the 1940s that the Queen Mother, Queen Kossamak, brought men into the royal ballet troupe to play the distinctive animal role of monkeys.

CLASSICAL DANCE

Recently, as part of a story I was shooting for the *Smithsonian Magazine*, I spent some time with one of the dance troupes in Siem Reap. Here, where booming tourism was bringing decidedly mixed blessings to the temples, it had been a boon for the revival of classical dance. The lengthy training, the costumes, instruments and the sheer numbers of dancers and musicians needed to put on a performance make it costly, but there are ready audiences in the evenings in some of the larger hotels and restaurants.

This was the Vat Bo dance troupe, founded in 1991 by a former member of the Royal Ballet in Phnom Penh. The school was a single-storey building just behind the monastery after which it was named, in a quiet district of town, winding dusty lanes, partly shaded by trees and palms. The classroom was a spacious extension on the corner, opening on to the lane – as of course did every shop and enterprise in the community. The roof was corrugated iron, which made it stunningly hot in the summer, when I first visited. Even with two fans fixed to a ceiling beam and a stand fan at full speed in one corner, it was rather uncomfortable in the afternoon, when the lessons and practice took place, generally starting at 3 o'clock. Beads of perspiration grew on the foreheads and upper lips of some of the girls as they rehearsed almost-complete dances. These were fully trained dancers, performing most evenings at restaurants and hotels – Siem Reap's tourist industry made it a healthy town in which to raise a classical dance troupe.

The training is long and arduous, and the girls need to start very young if they are to reach the top level. The second time I visited the troupe was in February, the cool season drawing to a close, and two of the senior dancers were instructing fourteen local girls, their ages ranging from eight to fifteen. The instruction was provided at no charge to the families, most of whom were too poor in any case to afford such unproductive tuition. And two of the trainees were orphans. All these girls were free to come and go as they pleased, and were under no obligation to continue with the Vat Bo troupe. That was the system, and indeed some of the girls did leave and join other troupes.

They had been training, more or less as a group, for just two months, which meant that there were many mistakes, and the two senior girls were constantly jumping up to correct a posture, a hand position, sometimes quite roughly. The classroom was much cooler than in the summer, but the dry season meant that whenever a motorcycle raced past, a light plume of dust flowed through the open doorway. Two of the trainees were quite clumsy, which was obvious even to an untrained eye, and were receiving a lot of attention, some of it exasperated. By contrast, one tiny girl was highly accomplished. I assumed that she was about seven, and was surprised at her skill, but one of the instructors later told me that she was ten years old, very small for her age, something you used to see in the old days because of insufficient food. Her movements were smooth and assured, her body still and her face composed. She was never corrected.

Changes of posture were signalled by one of the two instructors slapping a wooden stick full length on the linoleum floor. The musical accompaniment was provided by a boy on a *roneat* – a kind of xylophone with wooden keys suspended in a boatlike frame. The sound was much more melodious than you would have expected from wooden slats, and it did the job perfectly well by itself, with just the occasional help from a small drum

Village musicians at a temple ceremony

called a *skor*, and sometimes the voices of the dancers. They knew some of the words of some of the songs that accompanied dances, but more often they just sang 'noi, noi-noi . . . .'

After an hour, the founder of the troupe, the *kru*, or teacher, arrived – Neak Srei Hieng. She immediately apologized for the girls' dress, which was whatever they could find. The correct practice costume is a tight short-sleeved top in white, and a kind of pantaloon made by wrapping a metre-length of blue cloth round the waist and thighs, then gathering the ends and pulling them between the legs, securing everything with a silver belt. It was expensive, and the school would have to provide it since the girls' families were too poor. I had the impression that things were rather hand to mouth for the troupe, but even in the slowly improving Cambodian economy, this was not unusual. The week after my last visit, the troupe had toured Japan at the invitation of some private Japanese sponsors. I asked how it had gone. Very well, the *kru* replied, and they had danced in five cities, but at the end they had earned only US $45 because the sponsors had spent so much on the expense of flying them there and moving them around.

She broke off to call out to one of the instructors, gesturing at a girl in a yellow blouse and black skirt in the front row, 'Get her to stop waving her hips around!' The trunk has to remain decorous, glide when in forward movement, and certainly not gyrate. The girl, who was sixteen, was reacting to the rhythm as any teenager might, and this was not at all what was wanted. Quite the opposite, in fact. The instructor spent most of the next ten minutes kneeling behind the girl, tugging down on her hips and trying to hold them still.

Slowly and precisely, the dancers moved from one elegant but strongly flexed position to another. I wanted to use the word contorted, but this suggests awkwardness, and somehow the girls' hyperextended limbs bent and rotated into lines that appeared quite natural – for an otherworldly being, that is. This was precisely the intended effect. Long practice at bending joints into extreme positions, and holding them, helped to create magical, alien characters. By comparison, most Western dance is

184

positively acrobatic. The figures in classical Cambodian ballet are more weighted. The body as a whole moves less, but the individual parts, right down to the fingers and the eyes, are in constant, complex motion.

Depending on which combinations you count as separate, there are, it seems, between 1,500 and 4,500 positions. Memorizing these and moving from one to another in the correct sequence takes years of training. Like so many things Cambodian, all is not immediately obvious. The complexity is not displayed as it might be on a Western stage. The tension in the muscles, the strange displacements of gravity, the subtlety of a dozen or so actions taking place at once, are all tightly controlled, internalized.

The hand gestures alone are a study in form and symbolism, with several core positions, *kbach*, named after plants, including *kbach cheap* (flower), *kbach coung* (fruit), *kbach sung luc* (leaf) and *kbach chung aul* (bud or sprout). Each has not one, but several meanings, depending on the context and on how they are combined with other body and limb positions.

The *kru* rose to her feet to lead the young girls through the Dance of the White Dove, explaining the sequence of hand gestures. One set of three ends with the bud or sprout position, in which the second, third and fourth fingers are curled under an outstretched index as the hand is flicked over to one side. 'No!' she said, 'don't point down. This is about a celestial maiden [*srei suor tan*] and that's the direction of hell!' The senior girls laughed.

AT PREAH KHAN

On an August afternoon, I arranged for the troupe – two dozen dancers and the *pin peat* ensemble – to dance at the twelfth-century temple of Preah Khan. The choice of location was deliberate. This and a few other large temples built by Jayavarman VII, including Ta Prohm nearby and Banteay Chhmar in the northwest of the country (the scene of the looting saga), have a distinctive large building on their eastern side. Two features set these structures apart and led the French archaeologists to identify them as halls for dance performances. One is that the friezes at ceiling height all show rows of *apsaras* dancing in unison. The other is that, by the standards of Khmer stone architecture, they have fairly spacious interiors. This is relative, because the Khmers either never knew how to construct an arch or never felt the need for it. As a result, there are no great spans in even the grandest temples, just the narrow galleries that you can achieve by corbelling – jutting stones out from each wall, a little bit more with each successive course until they meet in the middle. The special Halls of Dancers gain their span by rows of pillars, and the performances would have taken place around these.

Preah Khan is being restored in a deliberately low-key way, slowly and with traditional technology, which means for the most part with a pulley, rope and chain. As a result, it remains one of the most pleasant monuments to visit, having avoided the industrial work-site atmosphere of some others. The Hall of Dancers is still only partly rebuilt, some fallen blocks here and there, and open to the sky. We all arrived early in the afternoon, since the lengthy preparation of make-up and costume would take place among the pillars.

As the girls helped each other with their gilded costumes, adjusting their ornate head-dresses, they came more and more to resemble the dancers carved above them. There was little, apart from the occasional plastic bag, that would have been out of place eight centuries ago, although twenty-first-century modesty required that the breasts, amply featured in stone, now be covered. But no one knows exactly what dances were performed here, and to what music. All that remain are snapshots in stone of a few poses, and some bas-reliefs of musicians playing recognizably the same instruments as today. There is no evidence that the *Ramayana*, in either Khmer or Sanskrit, formed part of the repertoire.

In fact, while the dance tradition clearly extends back to Angkor, it was King Duang, coming to the throne in 1848, who appears to have revived the classical court dance and directed it toward the way it looked in these twelfth-century Angkor

The Apsara Dance performed in the Hall of Dancers at Preah Khan

The Vat Bo classical dance troupe: rehearsals at the Siem Reap school

carvings. Until the early twentieth century, however, the royal dance troupe led a highly secluded life. Their performances were for the king alone, usually as an accompaniment to rituals, and indeed many of the dancers were also his consorts. Under the French, things began slowly to change, because dances were laid on for official occasions that involved the foreigners. Gradually, performances became more public. With the accession to the throne of Norodom Sihanouk in 1941, dancers were allowed to live outside the palace and to marry, while the Queen Mother brought male performers into the troupe and encouraged the creation of new dances to add to the repertoire. The Apsara Dance now about to be performed for me on this sultry afternoon was the most famous of these new pieces.

The central aisle of the roofless hall was reserved for the dance, right on the long axis of the temple. The musicians had arranged themselves behind and between two stone pillars on the right, off-stage as it were. This was the *pin peat* ensemble, the traditional accompaniment, all except one instrument percussion. As in the rehearsals, there was the xylophone-like *roneat*, but now two of these, one with sixteen wooden keys, the other with twenty-one. In addition, there was a *kong*, an almost-complete circle of small brass gongs mounted in a low rattan frame, and cowhide drums and cymbals. The only wind instrument is the *sralai*, like an oboe, and when the group strikes up, led by the large barrel drum, this adds a keen, piercing note to the bubbling percussion.

The troupe's lead dancer glides into the centre of the aisle, a golden *apsara*. Her movements, slow and deliberate, have a ritual quality, and evolve into the poses portrayed in the bas-reliefs. This was the intention of the choreographers of the Royal Court. She is joined by four of the other senior dancers. In unison, they reach the flying position, one leg raised behind, bent at the knee, the sole facing heavenward. This is just as the *apsaras* at Angkor Wat are first created by the Churning of the Sea of Milk, and fly high above the heads of Vishnu, the gods and demons.

Through the camera, the whole scene, with the crumbling temple falling away behind the girls, looks impossibly exotic.

189

When the Cambodian ballet was first seen in Europe in 1906, it must have seemed just as strange and exciting, and I remember years ago hearing about this. Around the time that I witnessed the ritual slaughter of the buffalo, Fred Grunfeld was beginning work on his classic biography of the sculptor Auguste Rodin. Fred was also writing the book on the hill-tribe that I was photographing, and we had endless hours with nothing to do but talk. Rodin, he told me, had not only seen the Cambodian royal ballet, but had been completely smitten by the dancers, executing in a number of days a series of drawings that were exhibited the following year. As Fred explained, the episode revived Rodin's interest in oriental art.

The occasion was the visit of the newly crowned King Sisowath and his court to France, an event encouraged by the French to spice up the Colonial Exhibition being held in Marseilles. His retinue numbered more than 100, of whom some 40 were the young dancers and a dozen musicians. For the French public these were the great exotic attraction, and in the following month the entire court moved up to Paris. The first performance was held at the Elysée palace, followed by another in the Bois de Boulogne. This was where Rodin saw them, and *Le Figaro* reported seeing 'the great Rodin, ecstatic beside Valentine de Saint-Point, the vestal-elect of his new fervour, go into ecstasies over the little virgins of Phnom Penh, whose immaterial silhouettes he drew with infinite love . . .' Another writer, Xavier Paoli, noted the dancers' unconventional, otherworldly appeal:

With their hard and close-cropped hair, their figures like those of striplings, their thin, muscular legs like those of young boys, their arms and hands like those of little girls, they seem to belong to no definite sex. They have something of the child about them, something of the young warrior of antiquity and something of the woman. Their usual dress, which is half feminine and half masculine, consisting of the famous *sampot* worn in creases between their knees and their hips and of a silk shawl confining their shoulders, crossed over the bust and knotted at the loins, tends to heighten this curious impression.

But, in the absence of beauty, they possess grace, a supple, captivating, royal grace, which is present in their every attitude and gesture.

Rodin was immediately obsessed with these little girls and their strange repertoire. He talked his way into the villa where they were staying in the rue Malakoff, and spent every minute available over the next few days furiously sketching with a new intensity. Georges Bois, the fine arts delegate from Saigon, wrote that Rodin was 'feverishly excited and seemed thirty years younger thanks to this new outburst of enthusiasm'. Unusually patient for once, Rodin was forced to play the doting uncle to the young girls in order to keep their attention, and whenever his model of the moment lost interest, Bois continued:

> The maître calm and gentle, and always patient – since he was unwilling to lose any of the short time remaining before the royal party's departure – would again submit to her whims. One day Rodin placed a sheet of white paper on his knee and said to little Sap: 'Put your foot on this', and then drew the outline of her foot with a pencil, saying 'Tomorrow you'll have your shoes, but now pose a little more for me!' Sap, having tired of atomiser bottles and cardboard cats, had asked her 'papa' for a pair of pumps. Every evening – ardent, happy but exhausted – Rodin would return to his hotel with his hands full of sketches, and collect his thoughts.

When the troupe had to return to Marseilles and their duties at the Colonial Exhibition, Rodin simply followed them, in such a hurry that he omitted to take with him paper for sketching. 'I arrived on a Sunday', he said,

> and went to the Villa des Glycines [where the dancers were staying]. I wanted to get my impressions on paper, but since all the artists' material shops were closed I was obliged to go to a grocer and ask him to sell me wrapping paper on which to draw. The paper has since taken on the very beautiful grey tint

and pearly quality of antique Japanese silks. I draw them with a pencil in my hand and the paper on my knees, enchanted by the beauty and character of their choric dances. The friezes of Angkor were coming to life before my eyes . . . I loved these Cambodian girls so much that I didn't know how to express my gratitude for the royal honour they had shown me in dancing and posing for me. I went to the Nouvelles Galeries to buy a basket of toys for them, and these divine children who dance for the gods hardly knew how to repay me for the happiness I had given them. They even talked about taking me with them.

Rodin's obsessive interest was not misplaced. The drawings were a success, and three dozen of them were exhibited at the Galerie Bernheim the following year. The poet Rainer Maria Rilke wrote effusively to Rodin: 'Great and dear maître, you have entered far more deeply than you realize into the mystery of the Cambodian dances', adding: 'For me, these drawings were a revelation of the greatest profundity.'

I was back at Preah Khan, the sprawling twelfth-century ruin, in the Hall of Dancers. The monsoon rains had held off and the dance performance was drawing to a close, the percussive melody rising and falling from the musicians seated between the lichen-encrusted pillars. The five dancers were directly in front of me as I faced west down the long axis of the temple. Behind the gently bobbing headers of the lead dancer, a few metres from where I stood, I caught a glimpse of the central stupa, far off through the succession of galleries.

The girls each carried a small gilt pedestal bowl, filled with rose petals for this last dance, the *Chuon Por*, or Blessing Dance. The late afternoon sun suddenly broke through the heavy clouds, bathing the small colonnaded courtyard in a rich glow. The costumes sparkled in the sunlight. I realized that I was coming to the end of the roll of film, and kneeling, hurriedly rewound it, opened the camera back and put in a new roll, anxious that I might lose the final picture. At these moments I have a superstition – I never look up until the camera is ready again, in the belief that time will stand still and I will have missed nothing.

When I did look up, I was only just in time. The dancers had lowered themselves to the ground, holding the small bowls out in front of them. We were all kneeling together. As the music reached a crescendo, the girls gathered a handful of petals from the bowls, and threw them into the air towards me. They fluttered to the stone paving. For a moment, all was still, a glittering scene of red and gold against the grey and green of the ruins. Eight centuries compressed into one tableau, the old Buddhist university and the young Khmer dancers from a newly formed troupe. Eight centuries in which so much had happened to Cambodia, and so much of it for the worse. Preah Khan was one of the last monuments of a powerful empire; the girls had all been born after the overthrow of Pol Pot. Yet the two were connected by a thread of renewal. The temple was being slowly and affectionately rebuilt by hand – by Khmer hands – while the dancers were part of a spontaneous local effort to rebuild Khmer culture. For a moment there was a sense of harmony, or at least the possibility of harmony. The girls pressed their hands together in the gesture of *sompeah*. The dance had ended.

Bibliography

Becker, Elizabeth, *When the War Was Over* (New York, 1986)

Bizot, François, *The Gate* (London, 2003)

Bouillevaux, Charles-Émile, *Voyage dans l'Indochine (1848–1856)* (Paris, 1858)

Bowden, Tim, *One Crowded Hour: Neil Davis Combat Cameraman, 1934–1985* (Sydney, 1987)

Briggs, Lawrence Palmer, *The Ancient Khmer Empire* (Philadelphia, 1951)

Carney, Tim, *Kampuchea: Balance of Survival* (Bangkok, 1981)

Chandler, David, *A History of Cambodia* (Boulder, CO, 2000)

—, *Facing the Cambodian Past* (Chiang Mai, 1998)

Chou Ta-Kuan [now Zhou Daguan], *Notes on the Customs of Cambodia*, trans. Paul Pelliot and J. Gilman D'Arcy Paul (Bangkok, 1967)

Clémentin-Ohja, Catherine, and Pierre-Yves Manguin, *Un siècle pour l'Asie: L'École française d'Extrême-Orient, 1898–2000* (Paris, 2001)

Dagens, Bruno, *Angkor: La Forêt de pierre* (Paris, 1989)

Delaporte, Louis, *Voyage au Cambodge* (Paris, 1880)

Coedès, George, *The Indianized States of Southeast Asia* (Honolulu, 1971)

Freeman, Michael, *A Guide to Khmer Temples in Thailand and Laos* (Bangkok, 1996)

—, *Angkor Icon* (Bangkok, 2003)

—, and Claude Jacques, *Ancient Angkor* (London, 1999)

Greene, Graham, *Ways of Escape* (London, 1980)

Grunfeld, Frederic V., *Rodin: A Biography* (New York, 1987)

Higham, Charles, *The Civilization of Angkor* (Berkeley, CA, 2001)

Jacob, Judith M., *Introduction to Cambodian* (Oxford, 1990)

Jacques, Claude, and Michael Freeman, *Angkor: Cities and*

Temples, trans. Tom White (London, 1997)

Lair, Richard C., *Gone Astray: The Care and Management of the Asian Elephant in Domesticity* (Bangkok, 1997)

Lewis, Norman, *A Dragon Apparent* (London, 1982)

Loti, Pierre, *A Pilgrimage to Angkor*, trans. W. P. Baines and Michael Smithies (Chiang Mai, 1999)

Macdonald, Malcolm, *Angkor* (London, 1958)

Madsen, Axel, *Silk Roads* (New York, 1989)

Magidson, Mark, *Baraka: A Visual Journal* (Los Angeles, 1999)

Malraux, André, *The Royal Way*, trans. Stuart Gilbert (New York, 1935)

Maugham, W. Somerset, *The Gentleman in the Parlour* (London, 1930)

Nagashima, Masayuki, *The Lost Heritage* (Bangkok, 2002)

Ngor, Haing S., and Roger Warner, *A Cambodian Odyssey* (New York, 1987)

Osborne, Milton, *Sihanouk: Prince of Light, Prince Of Darkness* (Chiang Mai, 1994)

—, *River Road to China* (Singapore, 1996)

Pasuk, S., and Philip Stott, *Royal Siamese Maps: War and Trade in 19th-Century Thailand* (Bangkok, 2003)

Phim, Toni Samantha, and Ashley Thompson, *Dance in Cambodia* (Kuala Lumpur, 2002)

Pym, Christopher, ed., *Henri Mouhot's Diary* (Kuala Lumpur, 1966)

Richards, P. W., *The Tropical Rain Forest* (Cambridge, 1966)

Rooney, Dawn, *Angkor Observed* (Bangkok, 2001)

Roveda, Vittorio, *Preah Vihear* (Bangkok, 2000)

Schanberg, Sydney, *The Death and Life of Dith Pran* (New York, 1985)

Shawcross, William, *Sideshow* (London, 1986)

Suksri, Naengnoi, and Michael Freeman, *The Grand Palace* (Bangkok, 1998)

Swain, Jon, *River of Time* (London, 1996)

Syamananda, Rong, *A History of Thailand* (Bangkok, 1977)

The Tourist Guide to Saigon, Phnom Penh and Amgkor (Saigon, 1930; reprinted Bangkok, 1992)

Tonkin, Derek, *The Cambodian Alphabet* (Bangkok, 1991)

Vickery, Michael, *Cambodia, 1975–1982* (Chiang Mai, 1999)